Quizzes exert a strong hold over anyone with a lively and inquiring mind. This sequel to the very successful *Quintessential Quizzes* includes hundreds of fascinating questions, many with unexpected answers, and should intrigue, entertain and stimulate the whole family.

More Quintessential Quizzes is compiled by Norman Hickman, a native New Yorker, with adaptations by Ian Gillies, winner of the 'Top Brain' award of the BBC's 'Brain of Britain' competition. It is introduced by Irene Thomas, herself a former Brain of Britain and regular member of the Round Britain Quiz team. Good luck in your attempts to outwit them!

MORE QUINTESSENTIAL QUIZZES

A Collection of Curious Words, Derivations, Literary Allusions, and Little-Known Oddities of Fact and Fiction

NORMAN G. HICKMAN
Adapted by Ian Gillies
Foreword by Irene Thomas

London
UNWIN PAPERBACKS
Boston   Sydney

First published in Great Britain by Unwin Paperbacks 1983

Unwin® Paperbacks
40 Museum Street, London WC1A 1LU, UK

Unwin Paperbacks
Park Lane, Hemel Hempstead, Herts HP2 4TE, UK

George Allen & Unwin Australia Pty Ltd
8 Napier Street, North Sydney, NSW 2060, Australia

British Library Cataloguing in Publication Data

Hickman, Norman G.
    More quintessential quizzes.
1. Questions and answers
I. Title   II. Gillies, Ian
793.73   AG195
ISBN 0-04-793062-4

Set in 9 on 10 point Univers Medium
by V & M Graphics Ltd, Aylesbury, Bucks
and printed in Great Britain
by Cox and Wyman Ltd, Reading

FOREWORD

Ever since the day when Oedipus solved the riddle of the Sphinx, quizzes have fascinated everyone who has a lively and inquiring mind.

This book contains hundreds of intriguing questions, and some unusual answers which may cause many family arguments and much searching in reference-books to confirm half-remembered facts . . . like 'What was the name of Alexander the Great's horse?' ... 'Why is a boudoir so called?' ... or: 'Who wrote the words and music for "Stardust"?'. One of the categories I find most interesting is the one titled 'Who said it first?' ... it's full of things I *thought* I knew!

It's all good, clean fun, and has been admirably 'translated from the American' by Ian Gillies, who is an expert question-setter himself, besides being 'Top Brain' in the BBC's 'Brain of Britain' contest – a very rare and hard-won honour.

Irene Thomas

PUBLISHER'S NOTE

This book is based upon the one volume *The Quintessential Quiz Book* first published in the United States of America. It has been anglicised by Ian Gillies for publication in two books. Many of the original questions are retained and the publishers acknowledge with thanks all those individuals who helped Norman Hickman in compiling his book.

Thanks are due for permission to reprint from the following copyright material:

Belloc, Hilaire, 'On His Books', *Sonnets and Verse* (London: Gerald Duckworth & Co Ltd.). Reprinted by permission of A. D. Peters & Co. Ltd., London.

Churchill, Winston S., from *Painting as a Pastime* (London: Ernest Benn Ltd.). Reprinted by permission of Ernest Benn Ltd.

Housman, A. E., 'When I Was One and Twenty' and 'A Shropshire Lad', from authorised editions of *The Collected Poems of A. E. Housman* (New York: Holt, Rinehart & Winston, 1939, 1940, 1965. Copyright 1967–68 by Robert E. Symons). Reprinted by permission of Holt, Rinehart & Winston.

Nash, Ogden. 'The Pig', 'The Turtle', *Verses From 1929 On* (New York: Little, Brown & Co., 1933, 1940, 1930). Reprinted by permission of Little, Brown & Co.

Schickele, Peter. *The Definitive Biography of P. D. Q. Bach* (London: Cassell Ltd., 1978). Reprinted by permission of Cassell Ltd.

Thurber, James, Reprinted by permission of Mrs James Thurber for one cartoon caption copyright 1943 by James Thurber. Renewed 1971. From *Men, Women and Dogs*, published by Harcourt Brace Jovanovich. Originally printed in *The New Yorker*.

CONTENTS

ABBREVIATIONS

What do the following mean?

1. K.C.B.
2. I.N.R.I.
3. C.C.C.P.
4. D.V.M.
5. a.k.a.
6. F.F.V.
7. b.i.d.
8. Q.E.D.
9. N.O.C.D.
10. AWOL

ABBREVIATIONS

1. Knight Commander of the Most Honourable Order of the Bath.
2. Jesus of Nazareth, King of the Jews (Latin *Iesus Nazarenus Rex Iudaeorum*) *or* Emperor Napoleon, King of Italy (Latin *Imperator Napoleon Rex Italiae*).
3. U.S.S.R. In the Russian alphabet C is equivalent to the English S, and P to the English R. Thus C.C.C.P. in the English alphabet reads *Soyuz Sovetskikh Sotsialisticheskikh Respublik*.
4. Doctor of Veterinary Medicine.
5. also known as.
6. First Families of Virginia, self-styled leaders of Southern aristocracy.
7. twice a day (Latin *bis in die*) – generally used by doctors on prescriptions. 't.i.d.' is three times a day.
8. That which was to be demonstrated or proved (Latin *quod erat demonstrandum*). Q.E.D. is generally used to indicate the solution of geometric problems.
9. Not our class, dear.
10. Absent without leave. (Although *without* is one word, to abbreviate this phrase without the O would mean 'absent with leave'.)

ALIASES

Can you give the real names of the following?

1. George Eliot
2. Lenin
3. El Greco
4. Saki
5. Boz
6. Lewis Carroll
7. Mary Westmacott
8. Sebastian Melmoth
9. O. Henry
10. Hitler

ALIASES

1. Mary Ann Evans.
2. Vladimir Ilyich Ulyanov.
3. Domenikos Theotokopoulos.
4. Hector Hugh Munro, who took the name 'Saki' from the cup-bearer in the *Rubáiyát of Omar Khayyám*.
5. Charles Dickens. Boz was the nickname of his younger brother.
6. Charles Lutwidge Dodgson, a mathematician at Oxford, where he wrote *Euclid and His Modern Rivals*.
7. Dame Agatha Christie, who was married to the archaeologist Sir Max Mallowan, used the name Mary Westmacott for her romantic novels.
8. Oscar Wilde used the name Sebastian Melmoth after his release from Reading Gaol. He chose Sebastian because of the arrows on the prison uniforms (St Sebastian was shot to death by arrows): Melmoth because one of his mother's kinsmen had written *Melmoth the Wanderer*, a famous novel of a man who had sold his soul.
9. William Sydney Porter, who spent three years in the Ohio Penitentiary for embezzlement. While there, he began writing short stories under a variety of pen names, including Oliver Henry, which later evolved into O. Henry.
10. Heidler, not Schicklgrüber. Hitler's grandmother was an unwed mother named Maria Anna Schicklgrüber. On the birth certificate of her son, Alois, the space for the father's name was left blank, and Alois went by the name Schicklgrüber until he was in his thirties. Before his son, Adolf, was born, though, Alois changed his name to Hitler, which was a variant of Heidler, the name of the man Maria Anna Schicklgrüber eventually married.

AMERICAN HISTORY

1. Can you name Columbus's first landfall?
2. Where was the first permanent English settlement in North America?
3. What was the name of the fort in the harbour of Charleston, South Carolina, whose bombardment marked the beginning of the Civil War?
4. Which general, who later became president, won a decisive victory after the war was over?
5. What took place in Philadelphia on 4 July 1776?
6. Do you know the two essential points of the Monroe Doctrine?
7. Against which president were impeachment proceedings brought?
8. Which Chief Justice did most by his decisions to fix the interpretation of the US Constitution?
9. In what year did the United States enter World War I, and who was President at the time?
10. Who made the decision to use the atomic bomb?

AMERICAN HISTORY

1. San Salvador, which most historians believe to be the island now also known as Watling Island, in the Bahamas.
2. Jamestown, Virginia, in 1607.
3. Fort Sumter.
4. Andrew Jackson, who defeated the British at New Orleans in the War of 1812 after peace had been signed in Europe.
5. The final draft of the Declaration of Independence was adopted, but not signed. The document was then engrossed on parchment, and all but six of the signatures were affixed on 2 August 1776.
6. The United States would not interfere in European affairs, and would view with displeasure any attempt by European powers to extend their political influence over the nations of the New World.
7. Andrew Johnson.
8. John Marshall.
9. 1917. Woodrow Wilson.
10. Harry S. Truman. (The S in his name does not stand for anything.)

ARCHAEOLOGY

1. Name the three ages which are commonly used in archaeological study.
2. Explain the importance of the Rosetta Stone, which was discovered in Egypt by Napoleon's troops in 1799 and is now in the British Museum.
3. With which areas of excavation are the archaeologists Heinrich Schliemann and Sir Arthur Evans associated?
4. Where are the sites of the ancient cities of Harappa and Mohenjo-Daro?
5. Who in 1922 discovered the fabulous tomb of King Tutankhamun in the Valley of the Kings, near Luxor, and who was his patron?
6. Can you describe a barrow and a kitchen midden?
7. In the eruption of Mt Vesuvius in AD 79, what was Pompeii covered with?
8. Name the supreme example of the Khmer temple building which was the meeting place of gods and kings and the deities' earthly home.
9. Which extraordinary ruin was discovered in 1911 by the American explorer Hiram Bingham?
10. Who in this century located in the Olduvai Gorge, Tanzania, a hominid fossil dating back over 1.7 million years?

ARCHAEOLOGY

1. The Stone, Bronze, and Iron Ages, referring to the material from which weapons and implements were made.
2. The Rosetta Stone, a basalt tablet with a decree of Ptolemy V written in Greek, Egyptian hieroglyphic, and demotic (a simplified form of ancient Egyptian hieratic writing), provided the key to deciphering hieroglyphics by Champollion and others.
3. Schliemann with Troy, Evans with Crete.
4. In the Indus valley in Pakistan.
5. Howard Carter. The fifth Earl of Carnarvon.
6. A barrow is a burial mound usually covered with earth, while a kitchen midden is a prehistoric refuse dump containing shells, bones, and artifacts.
7. Cinders and ashes, not lava.
8. Angkor Wat, in Cambodia. It is probably the largest religious structure in the world.
9. Machu Picchu, the fortress city of the ancient Incas, located high in the Peruvian Andes.
10. Dr Mary D. Leakey, wife of the famous archaeologist and anthropologist, Dr Louis Leakey, and mother of anthropologist Richard E. Leakey.

THE BIBLE

1. Name the first five books of the Old Testament.
2. Of what were Adam and Eve forbidden to eat in the Garden of Eden?
3. What is the shortest verse in the Bible?
4. In the Parable of the Ten Virgins, what were the five foolish virgins guilty of neglecting?
5. Four words appeared on the wall at Belshazzar's feast. What were they, and what did they signify?
6. In Biblical usage, what can the verb 'know' signify?
7. When 'the voice of the turtle is heard in our land', what time of year is it, and what is the turtle?
8. According to the Bible, how many wise men, or Magi, came from the east to Jerusalem to see the newborn Jesus?
9. Where did Noah's ark come to rest?
10. Who was given custody of the body of Jesus following the Crucifixion?

THE BIBLE

1. Genesis, Exodus, Leviticus, Numbers, Deuteronomy.
2. 'Of the tree of the knowledge of good and evil.' – Genesis 2:17.
3. 'Jesus wept.' – John 11:35.
4. They did not fill their lamps with oil. Hence, they could not welcome the wedding party and had to go forth into the darkness. The parable teaches the lesson of spiritual preparedness.
5. *Mene, mene, tekel, upharsin*, Aramaic words whose meaning is still uncertain. They may signify 'numbered, numbered, weighed, divided'. – Daniel 5:25. Daniel interpreted the phrase to mean that God had doomed Belshazzar's kingdom.
6. To have carnal knowledge of, to have sexual intercourse with.
7. Spring. The turtledove.
8. There is no number given. Matthew 2:1 simply says, '... there came wise men from the east to Jerusalem.' Christian tradition, however, has elaborated upon the biblical account: it has set their number as three, perhaps from their gifts of gold, frankincense, and myrrh; it has called them kings; and it has given them names – Caspar, Melchior, and Balthazar.
9. Not on Mount Ararat, but, according to Genesis 8:4, on 'the mountains of Ararat', the reference being probably to the mountain range rather than to any particular peak.
10. Joseph of Arimathea. According to legend, he founded the first Christian Church in England, at Glastonbury.

BIG AND LITTLE

1. Frances Hodgson Burnett devoted herself to the peerage in which novel?
2. Name two islands that are separated by an international boundary line and the International Date Line.
3. Which keen archer had a stature that belied his nickname?
4. Big Bertha, the large cannon used by the Germans in World War I, was named after whom?
5. Who observed that one would have to have a heart of stone to read about the death of Little Nell without laughing?
6. What do the Americans usually call the cluster of seven stars also known as the Plough?
7. Part of which former Welsh county is sometimes called 'Little England beyond Wales'?
8. Who created the enigmatic Chinese detective Charlie Chan?
9. Why did Fats Waller hate someone?
10. What was the name of the Antarctic base that Richard E. Byrd established in 1929?

BIG AND LITTLE

1. *Little Lord Fauntleroy*.
2. Big Diomede and Little Diomede, which lie in the Bering Strait between the U.S.S.R. and the United States.
3. Little John, in the legends about Robin Hood.
4. Bertha Krupp von Bohlen und Halbach, proprietress of the Krupp Works, where the cannon was made. (The German term was *dicke Bertha*, or Fat Bertha.)
5. Oscar Wilde.
6. The Big Dipper.
7. Pembrokeshire, the southern half of which is English-speaking.
8. Earl Derr Biggers.
9. 'I hates you, 'cause yo' feet's too big.'
10. Little America.

BIRDS

1. What famous comic dramatist wrote *The Birds*?
2. What 'perched upon a bust of Pallas just above my chamber door,' and what did it say?
3. What is the only bird that provides us with leather?
4. Who wrote the following to whom?

   > 'Hail to thee, blithe spirit!
   > Bird thou never wert.'

5. Can you explain the supposed connection between the goose and the soft, sheer, gauzy fabric known as gossamer?
6. Which unpleasant bird often hunts when he is not hungry and impales his prey on long, sharp thorns to keep it in reserve for a rainy day?
7. Which bird, with the largest wing span of any living bird, was prominent in what famous poem by whom?
8. Why is the missel thrush sometimes known as the storm cock?
9. Why is it illegal to shoot swans on the River Thames?
10. Collective nouns, as applied to birds and beasts, were first used in the sport of venery (used here in the sense of hunting, not lechery). How many of the following can you fill in with the correct noun of assembly?

    a) A.....................of quails
    b) A.....................of peacocks
    c) A.....................of finches
    d) A.....................of starlings
    e) An..................of larks

BIRDS

1. Aristophanes.
2. Poe's Raven. 'Nevermore.'
3. The ostrich.
4. Percy Bysshe Shelley, 'To a Skylark'.
5. Gossamer is said to be derived from 'goose summer', that time of year, corresponding to Indian summer, when the goose is in season and a fine film of cobwebs is often seen floating in the air or caught on bushes or grass.
6. The shrike, or butcherbird.
7. The albatross, which has a wing span of over ten feet (three metres), can soar for hours without beating its wings. 'The Rime of the Ancient Mariner', by Samuel Taylor Coleridge.

   > 'God save thee, ancient Mariner!
   > From the fiends, that plague thee thus! –
   > Why look'st thou so?' – 'With my cross bow
   > I shot the Albatross.'

8. Because it sings in all weathers, often perching on some high point and singing into the teeth of a gale.
9. Because they are the property of the Sovereign, and of two of the Companies of the City of London, the Dyers and the Vintners.
10. a) bevy
    b) muster
    c) charm
    d) murmuration
    e) exaltation

THE BRITISH ISLES

1. What are the longest rivers of England and Wales, Scotland and Ireland?
2. Where is London's geographical centre, from which all distances to and from the capital are measured?
3. How are the following place names pronounced?

   a) Fowey
   b) Belvoir
   c) Leominster
   d) Cobh

   e) Milngavie
   f) Ulgham
   g) Kirkcudbright
   h) Mousehole

4. Which four counties used to meet at the Four Shire Stone?
5. What isolated, uninhabited small island was annexed by Britain in 1955, and now administratively comes under the Western Isles Region of Scotland?
6. What are the names of the three National Parks in Wales?
7. Which English county had its name changed when local government was re-organised in 1974, but reverted to its former name in 1980?
8. What is the most southerly point of the English mainland?
9. Name the six counties that make up Northern Ireland.
10. Which landholder owns the most land in the United Kingdom?

THE BRITISH ISLES

1. The Severn (220 miles – 354 km), the Tay (117 miles – 188 km), and the Shannon (240 miles – 386 km), respectively.

2. The site of the statue of Charles I at Charing Cross, on the south side of Trafalgar Square. This was the location of the original Charing Cross, a replica of which may be seen in front of Charing Cross station.

3. The correct pronunciations are:

   a) foy
   b) beever
   c) lem-ster
   d) cove
   e) mil-guy
   f) uff-am
   g) ker-koo-bri
   h) moo-zel

4. Gloucestershire, Oxfordshire, Warwickshire, and Worcestershire. In 1931 some outlying Worcestershire territory was transferred to Gloucestershire, and now only Gloucestershire, Oxfordshire and Warwickshire meet at the Stone.

5. The aptly-named Rockall, which lies in the Atlantic north-west of Scotland.

6. The Brecon Beacons, the Pembrokeshire Coast, and Snowdonia.

7. Shropshire, which from 1974 to 1980 was officially known as Salop.

8. Lizard Point, in Cornwall.

9. Antrim, Armagh, Derry, Down, Fermanagh, and Tyrone.

10. The Forestry Commission.

BUSINESS AND FINANCE

1. What common piece of furniture lends its name to a bank?
2. How did the Stock Exchange terms of a bull, for an optimistic buyer, and a bear, for a pessimistic seller, supposedly come into being?
3. Why does the word *nepotism*, or the practice of favouring relatives with jobs, have an ecclesiastical origin?
4. What was the origin of the sign of three gold balls over pawnshops?
5. Can you describe the South Sea Bubble?
6. The term *A–1* for first-rate was originally used in what type of business?
7. Who scored a great financial success as a result of the Battle of Waterloo?
8. A salary was originally an allowance given to Roman soldiers to buy what?
9. Securities, generally thought of as stocks and bonds, should, by derivation, be carefree. Why?
10. Special Drawing Rights (SDRs) are a type of international monetary reserve established by which agency?

BUSINESS AND FINANCE

1. A bench, where the earliest money-changers conducted their business. The Old Italian word for bench is *banca*, from which we get the modern word 'bank'.
2. From the fighting characteristics of these beasts. When a bull attacks, he lifts you up on his horns. When a bear attacks, he claws you down.
3. Nepotism derives from the practice of the mediaeval Popes, who often conferred special favours and ecclesiastical offices upon their 'nephews' (Latin *nepotes*).
4. They are on the coat of arms of the Medici, early bankers.
5. A popular name for speculation in the South Sea Company, which in the early part of the eighteenth century had a monopoly of British trade with the islands of the South Seas and South America. It failed disastrously in 1720.
6. In the insurance business, particularly at Lloyd's of London, where the condition of a ship was so designated, the letters for its hull and the numbers for its equipment. (Lloyd's is named for Lloyd's Coffee House, in London, where marine underwriters used to meet.)
7. Nathan Rothschild, who was the first to receive the news – by carrier pigeon.
8. Salt.
9. Such investments are named from the Latin words *se* and *cura*, which are literally translated 'free from care'.
10. The International Monetary Fund, an intergovernmental agency of the United Nations.

CAPITALS

1. Name four national capitals that are planned cities.
2. Of which state is Tallinn the largest city and capital?
3. What and where is the Potala?
4. Where did Karl Marx do most of the research for his monumental *Das Kapital*?
5. Which national capital was once known variously as Edo, Yedo or Yeddo?
6. Near which capital are the ruins of ancient Carthage located?
7. Can you name a modern poet who eschewed capitals and who was, according to a publisher's note, 'the terror of typesetters, an enigma to book reviewers, and the special target of all the world's literary philistines'?
8. Which is the only street in London, not a one-way street, where one drives on the right?
9. Give the meaning of the word Acropolis as in Athens.
10. Who was mainly responsible for the replanning and rebuilding of Paris under the Emperor Napoleon III?

CAPITALS

1. Washington, D.C., U.S.A.; Canberra, Australia; Brasilia, Brazil; New Delhi, India.
2. Estonia, now a republic of the U.S.S.R.
3. It is the gigantic palace built for the Dalai Lamas, located in Lhasa, the capital of Tibet.
4. In the reading room of the British Museum in London.
5. Tokyo, Japan.
6. Tunis, Tunisia.
7. e. e. cummings.
8. Savoy Court, off the Strand, leading to the Savoy Theatre and Savoy Hotel.
9. High town, from the Greek *akros*, high, and *polis*, city.
10. Baron Georges Eugène Haussmann.

CATS AND DOGS

1. What is unique about Manx cats, and where did the breed originate?
2. Who was Cerberus?
3. Who described the archcriminal cat in these terms?
   Macavity's a Mystery Cat; he's called the Hidden Paw –
   For he's the master criminal who can defy the Law.
   He's the bafflement of Scotland Yard, the Flying
      Squad's despair:
   For when they reach the scene of crime – *Macavity's
   not there!*
4. Who were the respective owners of Diamond, Flush, and Toto?
5. Can you give the origin of the phrase 'not enough room to swing a cat'?
6. According to the US Public Health Service, what are the three breeds of dog that bite the least? The most?
7. What was the name of the fictional cat who suddenly showed a surprising ability to understand and speak the English language, and then proceeded thoroughly to unnerve a proper English houseparty by commenting acidly on the activities and characters of the various houseguests?
8. Weimaraner dogs were first bred in Germany for hunting stags in which peculiar fashion?
9. What are seal-points and blue-points?
10. What have mad dogs and Englishmen in common, according to whom?

CATS AND DOGS

1. Manx cats, which are practically tailless, came from the Isle of Man.
2. In ancient mythology Cerberus was the many-headed dog who guarded the gates of Hades.
3. T. S. Eliot, in *Old Possum's Book of Practical Cats*.
4. Sir Isaac Newton, Elizabeth Barrett Browning, and Dorothy, in *The Wonderful Wizard of Oz*.
5. This is a relic of the age of sail, when sailors were punished by means of a nine-thonged whip, called a 'cat-o'-nine-tails', which left welts like the scratches of a huge cat. Since there was 'not enough room to swing a cat' belowdecks, the punishment was administered topside.
6. Goldren retriever, Labrador retriever, and Shetland sheep-dog. German police dog (known in Britain as the German shepherd dog or Alsatian), chow and poodle.
7. Tobermory, in the short story of the same name by Saki (H. H. Munro).
8. They were trained to leap at a stag's genitals and rip them off.
9. Types of Siamese cats. Seal-points have a pale fawn coat, while blue-points have a grey one. Both types have darker ears, face, tail, and feet.
10. As Noël Coward said, 'Mad dogs and Englishmen go out in the midday sun.'

CHILDREN'S LITERATURE

1. Who were the other three members of the Outlaws, the gang led by Richmal Crompton's William?
2. Name the character whose first words every morning were 'What's for breakfast?'
3. In which novel did the ship *Hispaniola* play a large part?
4. Can you name the author of the Oz books?
5. In what book do Hazel, Bigwig, Blackberry and General Woundwort appear?
6. Who was Peter Pan's fairy? What was the name of the land where the children encountered mermaids, Redskins, and pirates?
7. Who wrote *Toad of Toad Hall*?
8. Which novel has been called the 'epic of American boyhood'?
9. For what is Sir John Tenniel most remembered?
10. What delightful fable was written by Antoine de Saint Exupéry?

CHILDREN'S LITERATURE

1. Ginger, Henry, and Douglas.
2. Winnie-the-Pooh in the A. A. Milne books.
3. *Treasure Island*, by Robert Louis Stevenson.
4. L. Frank Baum.
5. *Watership Down*, by Richard Adams.
6. Tinker Bell. Neverland (not Never-Never Land).
7. A. A. Milne. The play is based on Kenneth Grahame's book, *The Wind in the Willows*.
8. *Huckleberry Finn*.
9. The illustrations for *Alice's Adventures in Wonderland* and *Through the Looking-Glass*.
10. *The Little Prince*.

THE CINEMA

1. What was the first all-talking feature picture, and in what year did it appear?
2. Who said, 'Beulah, peel me a grape,' and in what film?
3. Who spoke the last words in *Gone With The Wind*, and what were they?
4. What did the films *Rebecca, The Great Man*, and *Edward, My Son* have in common?
5. Who played the part of the bank inspector, J. Pinkerton Snoopington, in the W. C. Fields film *The Bank Dick?*
6. Which actress was the top box office draw during World War II?
7. Can you complete the line 'Play ..., Sam' from *Casablanca*, and who said it? What was the title of the song referred to, and who played it?
8. One of the trademarks in films directed by Alfred Hitchcock is the walk-on nonspeaking appearance of Hitchcock himself. How did he accomplish this in *Lifeboat*, when the setting was a lifeboat holding the few survivors of a torpedoed ship?
9. Who is the only film star to appear on a European postage stamp?
10. A star's name is often made, not born. Do you know the screen names of the following:

    a) William Beedle
    b) James Stewart
    c) Norma Jean Mortensen
    d) Reginald Truscott-Jones
    e) Issur D. Demsky
    f) Frances Gumm
    g) Marion M. Morrison
    h) Anna Maria Italiano
    i) Frederick Austerlitz
    j) Allen Stewart Konigsberg

THE CINEMA

1. *Lights of New York*, in 1928.
2. Mae West, in *She Done Him Wrong*.
3. Vivien Leigh, as Scarlett O'Hara, closed the film, saying, 'After all, tomorrow is another day.'
4. The title characters never appeared on the screen.
5. Franklin Pangborn.
6. Betty Grable.
7. 'Play it, Sam.' (Not 'Play it again, Sam.') The words were spoken by Ingrid Bergman, not Humphrey Bogart. 'As Time Goes By' was played and sung by Dooley Wilson.
8. His picture was shown in a before-and-after slimming advertisement in a newspaper held by one of the survivors.
9. Grace Kelly, on the stamps of Monaco commemorating her marriage to Prince Rainier IV in 1956.
10.
    a) William Holden
    b) Stewart Granger
    c) Marilyn Monroe
    d) Ray Milland
    e) Kirk Douglas
    f) Judy Garland
    g) John Wayne
    h) Anne Bancroft
    i) Fred Astaire
    j) Woody Allen

CLUBS AND SOCIETIES

1. Can you name the four members of the Corresponding Society of the Pickwick Club?
2. Who described a club as 'an assembly of good fellows, meeting under certain conditions'?
3. Which London club is known as the In and Out?
4. What was 'The Red-Headed League'?
5. George Bernard Shaw's name is associated with which society, founded in 1883?
6. Of which club was P. G. Wodehouse's Bertie Wooster appropriately a member?
7. What was the Hell-Fire Club?
8. How many members are there in the Club of Rome, which was founded in 1968, and what are the objectives of the Club?
9. Who is reputed to have said, 'I wouldn't join any club that would have me as a member.'?
10. What did Charles Dickens's Mr Twemlow In *Our Mutual Friend* think was 'the best club in London'?

CLUBS AND SOCIETIES

1. Samuel Pickwick, Tracy Tupman, Augustus Snodgrass and Nathaniel Winkle.
2. Samuel Johnson, in his *Dictionary*. Dr Johnson described Boswell as a 'very clubable man'.
3. The Naval and Military Club in Piccadilly. 'IN' and 'OUT' are painted on its gateposts as a guide to vehicles entering and leaving the courtyard.
4. The title of one of A. Conan Doyle's Sherlock Holmes stories, in which the League was a ploy to ensure a successful bank robbery.
5. The Fabian Society, which was formed to promote the gradual spread of socialism. It was named after the Roman general, Quintus Fabius Maximus Verrucosus, called Cunctator (Latin, delayer), who defeated Hannibal by harassment and by avoiding direct confrontation.
6. The Drones.
7. A notorious eighteenth-century coterie, devoted to conviviality and debauchery, which included naked, masked women, weird religious rites, and drinking bouts. Among its members were Sir Francis Dashwood, John Wilkes, Charles Churchill, and the Earl of Sandwich. Benjamin Franklin was often a guest. The club first met in a ruined abbey and then in a series of immense caves on the Dashwood estate. These are now open to the public.
8. Membership is limited to one hundred and comprises humanists, scientists, educators, civil servants and managers from more than thirty countries. Its objectives are to probe the nature of world problems and to stimulate political action.
9. Groucho Marx.
10. The House of Commons.

COMMUNICATION

1. When Samuel F. B. Morse in 1844 demonstrated to Congress the practicality of the electric telegraph, what famous message did he transmit from Washington to Baltimore?
2. Britain has issued two £1 commemorative stamps, one in 1929 and the other in 1948. What event did each commemorate?
3. In Leigh Hunt's poem 'Abou Ben Adhem', what message did Ben Adhem give to an angel writing in a book of gold 'the names of those who love the Lord'?
4. What famous three-word alliterative phrase was borne in one of Caesar's triumphal processions following a great victory? In what present-day country did this battle occur?
5. What shape were the strokes used in cuneiform writing?
6. Does the international distress signal SOS mean 'Save Our Ship', 'Save Our Souls', or 'Stop Other Signals'?
7. To what did the Ems telegram lead?
8. Mayday, the international radio-telephone signal for aircraft and ships in distress, is the phonetic rendering of what?
9. 'Mr Watson, come here, I want you,' were the first words spoken into what?
10 Can you describe the 'Ultra Secret' of World War II?

COMMUNICATION

1. 'What hath God wrought!' – Numbers 23:23.
2. The Ninth Congress of the Universal Postal Union, held in London in May 1929, and the Silver Wedding of King George VI and Queen Elizabeth on the 26 April 1948.
3. 'Write me as one who loves his fellow men.'

   'The angel wrote and vanished. The next night
   It came again, with a great wakening light,
   And showed the names whom love of God had
      blessed,
   And lo! Ben Adhem's name led all the rest.'

4. 'Veni, vidi, vici' (I came, I saw, I conquered). In 47 BC Caesar defeated Pharnaces, King of Pontus, at Zela, which was located in north-east Asia Minor, now Turkey.
5. Wedge-shaped.
6. None of them. It is simply an easily remembered Morse Code signal of three dits, three dahs, and three dits. It was adopted by international agreement in 1912.
7. The Franco-Prussian War in 1870. The telegram described a meeting between the King of Prussia and a French representative. Bismarck altered the text to make it appear that there had been an exchange of insults, and released it to the Press.
8. The French *m'aider*, taken from a French version of a verse in the Psalms, which says '[Make haste] to help me [O Lord.]'
9. The prototype telephone. These were the words spoken by Alexander Graham Bell into his first telephone in 1876 to an assistant one room away.
10. The 'Ultra Secret', described as the outstanding crypt-analysis coup of the war, was the breaking of the German code by the British, who obtained from the Poles a precise copy of the complex coding machine known as Enigma. This enabled the Allies to intercept and read many German signals throughout the war.

CRIME AND PUNISHMENT

1. What is the origin of the term 'hoosegow'?
2. What is a 'paper-hanger'?
3. Early in nineteenth-century India a murderous religious sect flourished, whose members were known by the Sanskrit word *sthaga*. To what has this been anglicised?
4. In which section of London did Jack the Ripper operate?
5. Can you identify Javert?
6. Who invented the guillotine?
7. How did *Passer Domesticus* murder *Erithacus Rubecula*?
8. Which type of drug user is responsible for the word 'assassin'?
9. How did Scotland Yard get its name?
10. Name the authors who created the following fictional detectives:

   a) Nero Wolfe   f) Inspector Maigret
   b) Philip Marlowe   g) Sam Spade
   c) C. Auguste Dupin   h) Miss Marple
   d) Lord Peter Wimsey   i) Father Brown
   e) Roderick Alleyn   j) Ellery Queen

CRIME AND PUNISHMENT

1. From the Spanish word *juzgado* used in Mexico, meaning jail.
2. A passer of bad cheques.
3. Thug.
4. Whitechapel, in London's East End, where he gruesomely murdered at least five unfortunate drabs.
5. He appears in Victor Hugo's novel *Les Misérables* as a police officer in whom devotion to duty has crushed all human sentiment.
6. The guillotine was conceived of during the Middle Ages, but it was Dr Joseph Ignace Guillotin who advocated its use throughout France as a method of quick and painless death.
7. 'I', said the Sparrow. 'With my bow and arrow. I killed Cock Robin.'

   > 'All the birds of the air fell a-sighing and a-sobbing
   > When they heard of the death of poor Cock Robin.'

8. A marijuana, or hashish, user. In the olden Arabic days these people were called *hashshashin*, or hashish-eaters, from which assassin is derived.
9. Because it stood on the site of a palace where the Scottish kings once lived when they visited England.
10. a) Rex Stout
    b) Raymond Chandler
    c) Edgar Allan Poe
    d) Dorothy L. Sayers
    e) Dame Ngaio Marsh
    f) Georges Simenon
    g) Dashiell Hammett
    h) Dame Agatha Christie
    i) G. K. Chesterton
    j) Ellery Queen
    (Frederic Dannay and Manfred B. Lee)

CRICKET, RUGBY AND SOCCER

1. Who scored the first century to be made in any England–Australia Test Match, and in what year?
2. What is a Garryowen in Rugby?
3. Which English Football League clubs have the following nicknames:

   a) The Cottagers c) The Robins
   b) The Posh d) The Saints

4. In 1979 two counties, neither of which had ever won a major cricket competition before, both broke their ducks. Which counties were they, and what did each win?
5. Can you give the difference between the number of players in a Rugby League team and a Rugby Union team?
6. In the English Football League what are the four permitted colours for goalkeepers' jerseys?
7. What is a Chinaman in cricket?
8. In what match is the Calcutta Cup played for, and how did the Cup get its name?
9. Name the first British soccer team to win the European Cup.
10. Who wrote of 'the flannelled fools at the wicket or the muddied oafs at the goals'?

CRICKET, RUGBY AND SOCCER

1. Dr W. G. Grace, in 1880, at the Oval in the first Test ever played in England. He made 152, this being his first appearance for England, and the only occasion on which the three brothers Grace – E. M., W. G., and G. F. – all played together for England.
2. An 'up-and-under' – a high kick intended to land at the same time as a pack of charging forwards arrive at the spot.
3.   a) Fulham   c) Charlton
      b) Peterborough   d) Southampton
4. Essex won the Schweppes County Championship and the Benson and Hedges Cup. Somerset won the Gillette Cup and the John Player League.
5. Two. There are thirteen in a Rugby League team, fifteen in a Rugby Union team.
6. Scarlet, royal blue, white and royal green.
7. An off-break bowled by a left-arm bowler to a right-handed batsman.
8. In the annual England and Scotland Rugby Union match. When the Calcutta Club in India was disbanded in 1878 the rupees remaining in its bank account were melted down and the metal used to make the Cup.
9. Glasgow Celtic, in 1967.
10. Rudyard Kipling in 'The Islanders'.

DAYS AND DATES

1. In a speech before a session of the Joint Houses of Congress, President Franklin D. Roosevelt referred to 'a date which will live in infamy'. What was the date?
2. How many birthdays does the Queen have each year?
3. Why is 12 August referred to as 'the glorious twelfth' in England and Scotland?
4. Our names for the days of the week are derived from the Latin, Old Norse, and Anglo-Saxon. Without going into these ancient roots, can you tell for whom each day is named?
5. How did the ice cream sundae get its name?
6. In Shakespeare's *Julius Caesar* a soothsayer warns Caesar to 'Beware the ides of March.' To which day is he referring?
7. What does the *D* in D-Day stand for? In which war was the term first used?
8. What are the four English Quarter Days, and on what date does each fall?
9. What will be the first day of the twenty-first century?
10. When did we start to reckon time from a theoretical birthdate of Christ?

DAYS AND DATES

1. 7 December 1941, the date of the Japanese attack on Pearl Harbour.
2. Two. One is her actual birthday, in April, and the other is what is called her official birthday, on a Saturday in early June, which is celebrated by the colourful ceremony of Trooping the Colour.
3. The date marks the opening of the grouse-shooting season.
4. Monday, day of the Moon; Tuesday, day of Tiw (a god of war); Wednesday, day of Woden (chief deity); Thursday, day of Thor (god of thunder); Friday, day of Frigg (Woden's wife); Saturday, day of Saturn; Sunday, the day of the sun.
5. This concoction apparently first appeared in an ice cream parlour in Wisconsin, where it was served only on Sundays, hence the name. The 'ae' ending was undoubtedly added later to lend a touch of class to the dish.
6. 15 March, according to the old Roman calendar.
7. Day, so the term literally means 'Day-day'. It was first used in World War I to designate the start of the Allied offensive at Saint-Mihiel.
8. Lady Day (25 March), Midsummer Day (24 June), Michaelmas (29 September), and Christmas Day (25 December).
9. 1 January 2001. (This will become clear when you consider the fact that the first century ended on 31 December 100, which marked the passing of the first hundred years.)
10. Since the sixth century, when Dionysius Exiguus, a monk and chronologist, conceived the idea. Prior to that, time was based on the date of the founding of Rome by Romulus, which was traditionally set at 753 BC. This system was called *ab urbe condita,* or AUC – that is, from the founding of the city.

DRINK

1. In a 'bourbon and branch', what is 'branch'?
2. The initials D.O.M. appear on the label of every bottle of Benedictine. What do they mean?
3. For what should John Styth Pemberton, a pharmacist, be remembered?
4. Tabasco, the very hot sauce, takes its name from what?
5. Which types of spirit are correctly spelt whisky?
6. What is the chief ingredient of mead?
7. How did the expression 'mind your p's and q's' possibly originate?
8. What was the old Gaelic word, meaning 'water of life', from which the word 'whisky' is derived?
9. Who was the sage who observed the following?

> Candy
> Is dandy
> But liquor
> Is quicker.

10. 'Let's get out of these wet clothes and into a dry martini' was said by whom?

DRINK

1. Water, specifically 'branch water', such as water from a stream, creek, or brook – the 'branch' of a river.
2. *Deo Optimo Maximo* (L.), to God, the Best, the Greatest: motto of the Benedictines.
3. He concocted the original Coca-Cola mixture in Atlanta in 1886.
4. Tabasco, a state in Mexico, the source of the peppers originally used in the sauce.
5. Only Scotch and Canadian. Irish, bourbon, and rye are spelt 'whiskey'.
6. Honey.
7. From the custom in English pubs of listing the patrons' beer orders on a board marked p and q, for pints and quarts.
8. Usquaebach (one of several variants of the Gaelic).
9. Ogden Nash, 'Reflections on Ice-Breaking', from *Many Long Years Ago*.
10. Robert Benchley (*not* Dorothy Parker or Alexander Woollcott).

ENGLISH LITERATURE

1. Name the last and unfinished novel by Charles Dickens.
2. Shelley's poem 'Adonais' is an elegy on the death of whom?
3. What are considered to be the first full-length detective novels in English, and who was the author?
4. Can you identify the famous poem which was written under the influence of opium?
5. Which novelist of Polish parentage wrote in English?
6. What is wrong about these lines from Keats's sonnet 'On First Looking into Chapman's Homer'?

> 'Or like stout Cortez with eagle eyes
> He star'd at the Pacific – and all his men
> Look'd at each other with a wild surmise –
> Silent, upon a peak in Darien.'

7. Who introduced Sherlock Holmes to Dr Watson?
8. Which character 'lards the lean earth as he walks along'?
9. What was significant about the discovery of the Isham Papers in Malahide Castle, Ireland, early in this century?
10. In which poem did a nineteenth-century writer foresee air transport, air warfare, and the United Nations?

ENGLISH LITERATURE

1. *The Mystery of Edwin Drood*.
2. John Keats.
3. *The Woman in White* and *The Moonstone*, by Wilkie Collins.
4. 'Kubla Khan', by Samuel Taylor Coleridge.
5. Joseph Conrad.
6. Balboa was the first Spaniard to look out over the Pacific, not Cortez.
7. Young Stamford, whom Watson ran into at the Criterion Bar off Piccadilly Circus at a time when he was looking for lodgings. Stamford took Watson to St Bartholomew's Hospital, where Holmes was working in a chemical laboratory. See the opening of *A Study in Scarlet*.
8. Falstaff, in Shakespeare's *Henry IV*, Part 1.
9. A great mass of James Boswell's manuscripts – letters, journals, and other papers – came to light. Lt-Col Ralph T. Isham purchased these in 1927 and later sold them to Yale University.
10. 'Locksley Hall', by Alfred, Lord Tennyson, as shown in the following lines:

'For I dipt into the future, far as human eye could see,
Saw the Vision of the world, and all the wonder that would be;

Saw the heavens fill with commerce, argosies of magic sails,
Pilots of the purple twilight, dropping down with costly bales;

Heard the heavens fill with shouting, and there rain'd a ghastly dew,
From the nations' airy navies grappling in the central blue ...

Till the war-drum throbb'd no longer, and the battle-flags were furl'd
In the Parliament of Man, the Federation of the world.

EUROPEAN HISTORY

1. What empire was divided by the Treaty of Verdun?
2. For what exploit is Godfrey de Bouillon famous?
3. With the fall of what city in 1492 did the Moors lose their last foothold in Spain?
4. Who met on 'The Field of Cloth of Gold'?
5. Who transferred the capital of Russia from Moscow to St Petersburg early in the eighteenth century?
6. Which Italian family ruled Florence during Renaissance times?
7. Who crowned Napoleon at Nôtre Dame in 1804?
8. Who was sometimes known as the Uncrowned King of Ireland?
9. What event triggered World War I?
10. Why was 1 September 1939 a significant date?

EUROPEAN HISTORY

1. Charlemagne's empire, in 843. It was partitioned between his three grandsons Lothair, Louis the German and Charles the Bald.
2. His leadership of the First Crusade, from 1096 to 1100.
3. Granada.
4. Henry VIII of England met François I of France in 1520, on a field near Calais in company with the courts of both rulers. (The phrase 'Cloth of Gold' refers not to a carpeting, but to the colour of the tents. The meeting place is often erroneously referred to as 'The Field of the Cloth of Gold'.)
5. Peter the Great, so that Russia could have 'a window to the West'.
6. The Medici.
7. He crowned himself, although Pope Pius VII was present to perform that function.
8. Charles Stewart Parnell, who led the movement for Irish Home Rule from 1877 to 1890.
9. The assassination of the Archduke Franz Ferdinand of Austria at Sarajevo, Bosnia, in June 1914.
10. It marked the beginning of World War II, when Germany invaded Poland without a declaration of war.

FICTIONAL FAREWELLS

Name the character who uttered the following final words, which may or may not be dying words.

1. 'Rosebud.'
2. 'O, I am slain!'
3. 'For the love of God! Montresor!'
4. 'Mother of Mercy, is this the end of Rico?'
5. 'I've had such a curious dream!'
6. 'Thus with a kiss I die.'
7. 'Louis, I think this is the beginning of a beautiful friendship.'
8. 'What should I stay ...'
9. 'It is a far, far better thing that I do, than I have ever done; it is a far, far better rest that I go to, than I have ever known.'
10. 'Where am I? What am I doing? Why? God forgive me everything!'

FICTIONAL FAREWELLS

1. Charles Foster Kane (who was modelled on William Randolph Hearst and played by Orson Welles), in the film *Citizen Kane*. ('Rosebud' was the name on his boyhood sledge.)
2. Polonius, in Shakespeare's *Hamlet*.
3. Fortunato, in Poe's 'The Cask of Amontillado'.
4. Caesar Enrico Bandello (Edward G. Robinson), in the film *Little Caesar*.
5. Alice, in *Alice's Adventures in Wonderland*, by Lewis Carroll.
6. Romeo, in Shakespeare's *Romeo and Juliet*.
7. Rick Blaine (Humphrey Bogart), to Captain Louis Renault (Claude Rains) at the end of the film *Casablanca*.
8. Cleopatra, in Shakespeare's *Antony and Cleopatra*.
9. Sidney Carton, in *A Tale of Two Cities*, by Charles Dickens.
10. Anna, in Leo Tolstoy's *Anna Karenina*.

FLIGHT

1. How were the wings of a mythical ill-fated flier secured?
2. Where may the world's most famous winged statue be seen?
3. For what were the Montgolfier brothers famous?
4. Why is the date 17 December 1903 memorable in the annals of aviation?
5. Who was the top-ranking ace of World War I, and how many planes is he credited with shooting down?
6. What were merged in 1918 to form the Royal Air Force?
7. For what use was the tower of the Empire State Building originally intended?
8. Who gave this tribute to which force during World War II: 'Never in the field of human conflict was so much owed by so many to so few.'?
9. Can you identify the lady named as Enola Gay?
10. With the advent of supersonic flight, by what unit is the speed of supersonic aircraft measured? What does this unit mean?

FLIGHT

1. Icarus's wings were fastened with wax, which melted under the rays of the sun.
2. The 'Nike' or 'Winged Victory of Samothrace' may be seen in the Louvre Museum, Paris. Carved at the end of the fourth century BC, it commemorated a naval victory.
3. They invented the first practical man-carrying balloon, in France, in 1783.
4. That was the date when Orville and Wilbur Wright made the first controlled, sustained flights in a power-driven aeroplane near Kelly Hawk, North Carolina.
5. Manfred von Richthofen, nicknamed 'the Red Baron' because of the colour of the planes he flew, had eighty allied aircraft to his credit when he was killed in action in 1918.
6. The Royal Flying Corps and the Royal Naval Air Service.
7. For the mooring of airships, a plan which never proved feasible.
8. Prime Minister Winston Churchill, in a tribute to the Royal Air Force, in the House of Commons, August 1940.
9. She was the mother of Colonel Paul Tibbets, Jr., who commanded the B-29, named after her, that dropped the first atomic bomb on Hiroshima in 1945 and led to the Japanese surrender.
10. By Mach number. Mach 1 equals the speed of sound at a given altitude (approximately 760 mph at sea level and about 650 mph above 35,000 feet). Mach 2 is twice as fast. This system was named after Dr Ernst Mach, an Austrian physicist who had experimented with supersonics. Speeds between Mach 1 and Mach 5 are known as supersonic, and above Mach 5, hypersonic.

GAMES

1. What is the world's largest-selling game?
2. What game is sometimes said to have been invented by Harold S. Vanderbilt while on a Caribbean cruise in 1925?
3. In gambling casinos, which common object is generally missing?
4. Who was the compulsive gambler who wrote a novel entitled *The Gambler*?
5. 'Tables' and 'tric-trac' were the former names for what popular game?
6. The numbers on opposite sides of a die add up to what?
7. What game is played with pegs? With tiles?
8. Can you name the six pieces used in chess?
9. *The Art of Winning Games Without Actually Cheating* is the subtitle of what classic work on games?
10. What does the poker term 'dead man's hand' mean, and how did it originate?

GAMES

1. 'Monopoly'. More than 80 million 'Monopoly' games have been sold since 1935 when Parker Brothers bought it from its inventor, Charles B. Darrow.
2. Contract bridge.
3. There are no clocks to be seen, so as not to remind the patrons of the passage of time. For the same reason casinos have no windows.
4. Fyodor Dostoevsky.
5. Backgammon.
6. Seven.
7. Cribbage. Mah-jongg.
8. King, queen, rook (or castle), bishop, knight, and pawn.
9. *The Theory and Practice of Gamesmanship*, by Stephen Potter.
10. It is a pair of aces and a pair of eights together ('aces over eights'). This was the hand that Wild Bill Hickok was holding when he was shot from behind and killed in Deadwood, Dakota Territory, in 1876.

A GARDEN OF CURIOSITIES

1. The Greek goddess of the rainbow gives her name to what flower of varied and striking colours?
2. To what flower, with its sunburst centre and radiant petals, was Chaucer referring when he wrote 'the eye of day'?
3. Why is an anemone sometimes called a windflower?
4. What type of clover was used by St Patrick as his symbol?
5. Why does the dainty pansy wear such a 'thoughtful' mien?
6. Can you describe a desert rose?
7. For whom was the poinsettia named, and why is it considered an appropriate Christmas plant?
8. Where was the scene of the agony of Jesus?
9. Where did Monet paint his famous water lilies?
10. The name of what flower is derived from the Greek word for 'testicle', which it resembles because of its double roots?

A GARDEN OF CURIOSITIES

1. Iris.
2. The daisy.
3. Because its name derives from a word influenced by *anemos*, the Greek word for 'wind'.
4. The shamrock, which was supposedly used by St Patrick to illustrate the Trinity because of its three leaves.
5. Because its original name was *pensée*, French for 'thought', which developed into 'pansy'.
6. It is not a flower at all but a rock, consisting of grains of sand fused together, the surface of which has been eroded by the elements so that it resembles a rose. Desert roses are commonly found in the Sahara.
7. Joel Roberts Poinsett, of Charleston, South Carolina, who after a mission to Mexico, brought the plant with the large flaming leaves back to the United States. Poinsettias are favoured at Christmas because the leaves generally stay red until Easter.
8. The Garden of Gethsemane, outside Jerusalem.
9. In his garden at Giverny, France. It is being restored by the generosity of the Lila Acheson Wallace Foundation.
10. Orchid, from *orchis*, testicle.

THE GROVES OF ACADEME

1. Who advised us to 'seek for truth in the groves of Academe'?
2. When compulsory education was introduced in England and Wales in 1876, up to what age did a child normally have to attend school?
3. Who was the famous headmaster to whom Thomas Hughes paid tribute in *Tom Brown's Schooldays*?
4. Who educated whom at the 'College of One'?
5. Alexander the Great was fortunate in having whom as a tutor?
6. Can you name the five Oxford colleges each of which has exactly the same name as a Cambridge college?
7. Which is the oldest university in Scotland?
8. The 'School of the Ten Bells' specialises in which delicate craft?
9. Which leading university was named after an Englishman who had amassed a fortune with the East India Company?
10. What remarkably inept student wrote the following in later years?

   'By being so long in the lowest form I gained an immense advantage over the cleverer boys ... I got into my bones the essential structure of the ordinary British sentence – which is a noble thing. Naturally I am biased in favour of boys learning English; and then I would let the clever ones learn Latin as an honour, and Greek as a treat. But the only thing I would whip them for would be for not knowing English. I would whip them hard for that.'

THE GROVES OF ACADEME

1. Horace, in Book II of his Epistles.
2. Twelve, although there were provisions for exemption at an earlier age.
3. Dr Thomas Arnold, who was Headmaster of Rugby from 1828 to 1842, and was also the father of the poet Matthew Arnold.
4. F. Scott Fitzgerald instructed Sheilah Graham, who described the experience in her book *Beloved Infidel*.
5. Aristotle.
6. Pembroke, Corpus Christi, Jesus, St John's, and Trinity.
7. The University of St Andrews, founded in 1411.
8. It is a school for pickpockets. Its curriculum involves a mannequin with ten pockets in its clothing, on each of which a bell has been sewn. To graduate, the student must pick every pocket without ringing a bell.
9. Yale University, formerly the Collegiate School, changed its name in 1718 in honour of Elihu Yale, who had donated a gift of goods and books to the school. When sold, these brought £562 – the largest gift to the college before 1837. Although Yale died a rich man, he left nothing in his estate to the college which had honoured him. Elihu Yale is buried in Wrexham, Wales.
10. Winston S. Churchill in *My Early Life*.

HUMOUR

Can you identify the authors of the following?

1. 'Give a man a free hand and he'll run it all over you.'
2. 'The trouble with nude dancing is that not everything stops when the music stops.'
3. 'News is what a chap who doesn't care much about anything wants to read.'
4. 'I always wait for *The Times* each morning. I look at the obituary column, and if I'm not in it, I go to work.'
5. 'He flung himself from the room, flung himself upon his horse and rode madly off in all directions.'
6. 'If all the girls at the Yale Prom were laid end to end, I wouldn't be at all surprised.'
7. 'I was gratified to be able to answer him promptly, and I did. I said I didn't know.'
8. 'Yesterday morning I awoke from a deep dream of peace, compounded of equal parts of allonal and Vat 69, to find that autumn was indeed here.'
9. 'I believe a little incompatibility is the spice of life, particularly if he has income and she is pattable.'
10. 'A woman drove me to drink, and I never even had the courtesy to thank her.'

HUMOUR

1. Mae West
2. Sir Robert Helpmann
3. Evelyn Waugh
4. A. E. Matthews
5. Stephen Leacock
6. Dorothy Parker
7. Mark Twain
8. S. J. Perelman
9. Ogden Nash
10. W. C. Fields

HUNTING, SHOOTING AND FISHING

1. Name a great-grandson of Noah who was a mighty hunter.
2. Which sporting classic was written by Izaak Walton in the seventeenth century?
3. Doing a 'Macnab' is a difficult day's work. What does it involve?
4. If one hunting man was telling another hunting man he had seen twenty-seven foxhounds, how would he say twenty-seven?
5. Describe a capercaillie or capercailzie.
6. How did Francis Macomber die in Hemingway's story *The Short Happy Life of Francis Macomber*?
7. What is an arctic char?
8. Can you name the most popular gamebird in Spain?
9. What is the name of the narrator of Siegfried Sassoon's *Memoirs of a Fox-Hunting Man*?
10. Which famous book was reviewed in the following terms?

'This fictional account of the day-by-day life of an English gamekeeper is still of considerable interest to outdoor-minded readers, as it contains many passages on pheasant raising, the apprehending of poachers, ways to control vermin, and other chores and duties of the professional game-keeper. Unfortunately one is obliged to wade through many pages of extraneous material in order to discover and savour these sidelights on the management of a Midlands shooting estate, and in this reviewer's opinion this book cannot take the place of J. R. Miller's *Practical Gamekeeping*.'

HUNTING, SHOOTING AND FISHING

1. Nimrod – Genesis 19:8-10.
2. *The Compleat Angler, or the Contemplative Man's Recreation*. Besides describing the art of angling, Walton draws a picture of peace and meditation which is in sharp contrast to the civil war raging at the time.
3. Killing a salmon, shooting a grouse, and stalking and killing a stag within twenty-four hours. The term came from a feat described in the novel *John Macnab* by John Buchan in which the owners were forewarned that their lands would be poached.
4. Thirteen and a half couple.
5. It is a large grouse. Its name derives from a Scottish-Gaelic word meaning 'horse of the woods'.
6. He was shot by his wife after showing cowardice on safari by running away from a wounded lion.
7. It is a type of trout.
8. The *perdiz*, or red-legged partridge.
9. George Sherston.
10. *Lady Chatterley's Lover*, by D. H. Lawrence. This tongue-in-cheek review by Ed Zern appeared in the magazine *Field and Stream*.

INSULTS

1. Beau Brummell, encountering the Prince Regent and a companion out for a stroll in London, made what scathing enquiry of the companion?

2. Who described Algernon Charles Swinburne as 'sitting in a sewer and adding to it'?

3. What did Samuel Johnson have to say about the letters of Lord Chesterfield?

4. 'The same old sausage, fizzing and sputtering in his own grease' was whose opinion of Thomas Carlyle?

5. Walking down Piccadilly one day, the Duke of Wellington was addressed by a stranger who said, 'Mr Brown, I believe?' What was the Iron Duke's reply?

6. How did Winston Churchill handle Lady Astor when she said, 'If you were my husband, I'd poison your coffee.'?

7. George Bernard Shaw received this invitation from a celebrity huntress: 'Lady X will be at home Thursday between four and six.' He returned the card, having written what on it?

8. When they were leaving by the same door, Clare Boothe waved Dorothy Parker ahead, saying, 'Age before beauty.' Miss Parker swept through with what apt rejoinder?

9. Who is reputed to have said, 'I never forget a face, but in your case I'll make an exception.'?

10. In which fashion is Churchill supposed to have knifed Clement Attlee when someone observed that he was a very modest man?

INSULTS

1. 'Who's your fat friend?'
2. Thomas Carlyle.
3. The famous letters, Johnson found, teach 'the morals of a whore and the manners of a dancing master'.
4. Henry James.
5. 'Sir, if you believe that, you'll believe anything.'
6. 'And if I were your husband, I should drink it.'
7. 'So will Mr Bernard Shaw.'
8. 'Pearls before swine.'
9. Groucho Marx.
10. Churchill is said to have agreed, adding, 'He has a great deal to be modest about.'

JAZZ

1. Where was Storyville, and what part did it play in the early history of jazz?
2. Explain the term 'tailgate trombone'.
3. Who was the 'Empress of the Blues'?
4. Which prolific jazz musician held sacred music concerts in Grace Cathedral, San Francisco, and in the Cathedral of St John the Divine in New York?
5. Who has been called the 'King of Ragtime'?
6. Who was the first jazz man to recruit band members purely on the basis of musical ability, without regard for race?
7. Which famous jazz club was named after the father of modern jazz? Who was he?
8. What was unusual about the guitarist Django Reinhardt?
9. A new market for jazz as a concert form was exploited by which group? Who played alto saxophone?
10. Which singer has performed with virtually every major jazz musician?

JAZZ

1. It was the legendary red-light district of New Orleans, consisting of a 38-block area, where many of the early jazz bandleaders appeared in the sporting houses. Its closing by the Navy in 1917 had the effect of dispersing jazz musicians and their talents throughout the country.
2. This was the style of playing trombone in New Orleans and takes its name from the location of the trombonist on a horsedrawn parade cart, where he would have ample room to operate the trombone slide.
3. Bessie Smith.
4. Duke Ellington.
5. Scott Joplin.
6. Benny Goodman.
7. Birdland. Charlie 'Yardbird' Parker.
8. He had only three fingers on his left hand and was a gypsy.
9. The Dave Brubeck Quartet. Paul Desmond.
10. Ella Fitzgerald.

KITH AND KIN

1. Whose grandmother was eaten by a beast?
2. Who lived with Uncle Henry and Aunt Em?
3. What relation was Queen Victoria to King William IV whom she succeeded?
4. George McManus originated which famous comic strip, featuring a successful Irish immigrant and his parvenu wife?
5. Who wished his wife 'to be not so much as suspected'?
6. Can you name the March sisters of literature?
7. Who was the original Uncle Sam whose name became the national symbol of the United States, and what was his business?
8. Who stood on his head, somersaulted, devoured an entire goose, and balanced an eel on the end of his nose?
9. Which two ladies served poisoned elderberry wine to elderly gentlemen?
10. What was the real name of Uncle Mac of the BBC Children's Hour?

KITH AND KIN

1. Little Red Riding Hood, in the well-known tale translated from the French of Perrault.
2. Dorothy, in L. Frank Baum's *The Wonderful Wizard of Oz*.
3. She was his niece.
4. 'Bringing up Father', with Jiggs and Maggie.
5. Julius Caesar, according to Plutarch's *Lives*. This is the origin of the traditional saying that Caesar's wife must be above suspicion.
6. Jo, Meg, Beth, and Amy, in *Little Women*, by Louisa May Alcott.
7. Samuel Wilson, a meat-packer from Troy, New York, who was called 'Uncle Sam' by his employees. During the War of 1812, the initials 'US' stamped on food containers for the armed forces were jokingly said to stand for 'Uncle Sam'.
8. Father William, from the verse in Lewis Carroll's *Alice's Adventures in Wonderland*.
9. The Brewster sisters, Aunt Abby and Aunt Martha, in the play *Arsenic and Old Lace*, by Joseph Kesselring.
10. Derek McCulloch.

THE LAW

1. What is the difference between libel and slander at common law?
2. What is the title of the chief Law Officer of the Crown in Scotland?
3. What is *habeas corpus*?
4. Who proclaimed that 'the law is a ass – a idiot'?
5. Who was the MP for Oxford University whose novel *Holy Deadlock* helped to pave the way for a bill which he later promoted to reform the divorce law?
6. Can you state the substance of Parkinson's Law?
7. What are the names of the three divisions of the High Court of Justice?
8. What formerly was the distinction between burglary and housebreaking?
9. What is the offence of jactitation of marriage?
10. Murphy's Laws are justifiably famous. Can you give two out of three?

THE LAW

1. Libel is written, or mechanically broadcast, while slander is only spoken.
2. The Lord Advocate.
3. The writ issued to bring a person before a court or judge to determine that there has been no unlawful restraint.
4. Mr Bumble, in Charles Dickens's *Oliver Twist*.
5. A. P. Herbert, later Sir Alan Herbert.
6. Parkinson's Law states: 'Work expands to fill the time available for its completion.' This law was enunciated by Professor C. Northcote Parkinson in an article published in *The Economist* in London in 1955 after investigating the British Admiralty and the Colonial Office.
7. The Chancery, Queen's Bench, and Family Divisions.
8. Burglary was breaking into a house with intent to commit a felony between the hours of 9 pm and 6 am. Outside those hours it was called housebreaking. The 1968 Theft Act abolished the distinction, and the term burglary now applies throughout the twenty-four hours.
9. Falsely claiming to be married to someone.
10. Murphy's Laws have been codified as follows:

    a) Nothing is as easy as it looks.
    b) Everything will take longer than you think it will.
    c) If anything can go wrong, it will.

McMACS

1. As used in surnames, what do 'Mc' and 'Mac' indicate?
2. The abbreviation 'M.C.' might represent what six descriptive terms?
3. The resistance to the British bombardment of what fort inspired Francis Scott Key to do what?
4. Name an important body of water closest to the Ross Ice Shelf in Antarctica.
5. To which two men do we owe the names for a type of surfaced road and a raincoat?
6. Why is Ray A. Kroc one of the richest men in the United States?
7. In Japan a shogun was a military leader who exercised absolute rule. Who has been called 'the last shogun'?
8. Who said, 'Lay on, Macduff, /And damn'd be him that first cries, "Hold, enough!"'?
9. Which English historian and statesman was one of two powerful forces in shaping the distinctive prose style of Winston Churchill?
10. To Alfred Hitchcock, what is the MacGuffin?

McMACS

1. Son of.
2. Marine Corps, Medical Corps, Member of Congress, Military Cross, Master Commandant, or Master of Ceremonies.
3. The successful defence of Fort McHenry in Baltimore against the British naval assault in 1814 inspired Key to write what is now the American national anthem, *The Star-Spangled Banner*, on the morning following the bombardment.
4. McMurdo Sound.
5. John McAdam, a Scottish engineer, for the macadam road, which consisted of layers of compacted small stones, now usually bound with tar or asphalt; and Charles Macintosh, a Scottish chemist, who developed a raincoat of patented rubberised cloth.
6. He is the founder and Senior Chairman of the Board of the McDonald's hamburger chain.
7. General Douglas MacArthur, who from 1945 to 1951 was commander of the occupying forces of the Allied Powers in Japan and directed the occupation of the country.
8. Macbeth.
9. Thomas Babington Macaulay. The other strong influence on Churchill's style was Edward Gibbon, who wrote *The History of the Decline and Fall of the Roman Empire*.
10. The motive force in his films, or the 'secret' everyone is intent on either keeping or revealing.

MAGIC AND THE OCCULT

1. Can you explain the connection between the wise men from the East of the Nativity story and magicians?
2. How many cards are there in the tarot deck used in fortune-telling?
3. What is a familiar? Can you give the name of the familiar that appeared in John van Druten's play *Bell, Book and Candle*?
4. Name the prophetess in Greek legend whose predictions, though true, were never believed.
5. What are jumbies?
6. Do you know the legend of the witch who was nicknamed 'Cutty Sark'?
7. In what poem would you find these words?

    'It was down by the dank tarn of Auber,
    In the ghoul-haunted woodland of Weir.'

8. Who was Erich Weiss, and what was his contribution to magic?
9. Of what are the leprechauns of Ireland inordinately fond?
10. Complete the Scottish prayer which begins 'From ghoulies and ghosties'.

MAGIC AND THE OCCULT

1. The wise men were also called the Magi. This is the plural of the Persian word *magus*, or scorcerer, from which the word magician is derived.
2. Seventy-eight cards, 56 of which are called the *Minor Arcana* and the remaining 22 the *Major Arcana*.
3. An attendant spirit which often takes animal form. A Siamese cat called Pyewacket.
4. Cassandra, a daughter of Priam, King of Troy. Apollo, to woo her, imparted to Cassandra the gift of prophecy. Enraged when she rejected him, he could not retract the gift, but added the terrible qualification that she would never be believed.
5. To the natives of the West Indies, they are zombies, or the living dead.
6. In his poem 'Tam O'Shanter' Robert Burns tells of a country boy fleeing a pursuing witch who was clad only in a *cutty sark* (a short petticoat in Scots dialect). Knowing that witches cannot follow over water, he rode his mare over a bridge. Nevertheless, 'Cutty Sark' did succeed in snatching the mare's tail. The figurehead of Britain's famed tea clipper *Cutty Sark*, now preserved at Greenwich on the Thames, is a young woman in a cutty sark, with a mare's tail in her outstretched hand.
7. 'Ulalume', by Edgar Allan Poe.
8. Weiss was the real name of Harry Houdini, who took his stage name after the noted French magician Houdin. Houdini was a master in the art of escape and also exposed fake mediums.
9. Whiskey and tobacco.
10. 'And long-leggety beasties and things that go bump in the night, Good Lord, deliver us!'

MEETINGS

1. Who had a historic meeting at Ujiji?
2. Which representatives of the 'Big Three' (Great Britain, Russia and the United States) met at the Potsdam Conference in the summer of 1945, following Germany's defeat in World War II?
3. Where do the Society of Friends regularly get together?
4. These lines open which well-known play?

    'When shall we three meet again?
    In thunder, lightning, or in rain?'

5. Sherlock Holmes was destined to have his last meeting with his arch-enemy Professor James Moriarty at what spot on the Continent?
6. Who wrote, 'Oh, East is East, and West is West, and never the twain shall meet'?
7. What German phrase means 'Till we meet again'?
8. Where does the Blue Nile meet the White Nile?
9. Who was the author of the touching play *Still Life*, later made into a film called *Brief Encounter*?
10. Where do 'I have a rendezvous with Death,' according to Alan Seeger, a poet who achieved fame in World War I?

MEETINGS

1. It was here on the shores of Lake Tanganyika in 1871 that Henry Morton Stanley uttered the memorable words 'Dr Livingstone, I presume,' on encountering the famous Scottish missionary and explorer for whom he had been searching.
2. The successive Prime Ministers Churchill and Attlee, Marshal Stalin, and President Truman. (Attlee replaced Churchill as Prime Minister midway through the conference.)
3. At Meeting. The name 'Quaker' is probably derived from the admonition of George Fox, founder of the Society, to 'tremble at the word of the Lord'.
4. Shakespeare's *Macbeth*.
5. According to Dr Watson in 'The Final Problem', they last met on a precipice over the Reichenbach Falls, near Meiringen, Switzerland, where in the course of a struggle they both appeared to have fallen into the 'dreadful cauldron of swirling water', presumably to their deaths. Holmes, however, miraculously re-appeared to continue his adventures.
6. Rudyard Kipling, in 'The Ballad of East and West'.
7. *Auf Wiedersehen*.
8. The two great rivers have their confluence at Khartoum, the capital of the Sudan.
9. Noël Coward.
10. 'At some disputed barricade'. The poem ends as follows:

> 'But I've a rendezvous with Death
> At midnight in some flaming town,
> When Spring trips north again this year,
> And I to my pledged word am true,
> I shall not fail that rendezvous.'

MISTRESSES

1. Whose mistress was originally a peasant girl and later an empress?
2. Which king, when urged by his dying wife to marry again, said, *'Non, j'aurai des maitresses.'* (No, I shall have mistresses.)?
3. Why is the name Mayerling remembered?
4. Which British Prime Minister started his letters to his mistress, and later his wife, Frances Stevenson, with 'My Darling Pussy'?
5. Who became Napoleon's mistress in an attempt to save Poland?
6. The actress Marion Davies was the mistress of which famous newspaper publisher?
7. What was the occupation of Nell Gwynn, the paramour of Charles II?
8. Which wonderfully descriptive term has been applied to Emilienne d'Alçenon, Liane de Pougy, La Belle Otèro, and other *grandes cocottes* of *La Belle Époque*, as the decade of the 1890s in Paris was known?
9. According to Robert Service's poem, who worked at the Malamute saloon and was the light-o'-love of Dangerous Dan McGrew?
10. George Romney became famous for his protraits of the beautiful mistress of which celebrated naval commander?

MISTRESSES

1. Peter the Great, who married Catherine I of Russia.
2. King George II. Queen Caroline answered, '*Ah! mon Dieu! cela n'empêche pas.*' (My God, that is no obstacle.)
3. It was at a hunting lodge (now a convent) at Mayerling that Crown Prince Rudolf, heir to the Austro-Hungarian thrones and his mistress, Maria Vetsera, met their mysterious deaths in 1889.
4. Lloyd George.
5. Countess Maria Walewska.
6. William Randolph Hearst.
7. Once an orange-seller at the Theatre Royal, Drury Lane, she became an actress.
8. 'Grand Horizontals', whose affairs were described by Cornelia Otis Skinner in her book *Elegant Wits and Grand Horizontals*.
9. 'The lady that's known as Lou'.
10. Horatio, Viscount Nelson. Romney painted Emma, Lady Hamilton.

THE MONTHS OF THE YEAR

1. Which month is literally two-faced?
2. An epithet for Juno, the Roman goddess of marriage and fertility, gives us the name of which month?
3. How did the expression 'mad as a March hare' originate?
4. Why is April a perfect time for love?
5. The prologue of which famous work begins with these lines?

   'Whan that April with his shoures soote
   The droghte of March hath perced to the roote ...'

6. According to Sir Thomas Malory in *Morte d'Arthur*, which is the 'lusty month'?
7. In whose honour are June and July named?
8. Give the title of the best-selling book about World War I by Barbara W. Tuchman.
9. Walter Huston sang 'September Song' in which Broadway show, by whom?
10. September, October, November and December are literally the seventh, eighth, ninth, and tenth months respectively. How did this arise?

THE MONTHS OF THE YEAR

1. January, which comes from Janus, the Roman god for gates and doors, who was always represented on Roman coins as facing in two directions at once. This enabled him to gaze on both the past and the future at the same time.
2. February, from *Februaria*. At this time of year the Romans engaged in a curious celebration, which involved running around and striking women with sacred thongs so that they would not be barren. The name for these thongs was *februa*, or instruments of purification.
3. Because March is supposedly the mating season of hares, although some observers have noted that hares know no season. March is named after Mars, the Roman god of war, since the month was ideal for warfare.
4. Its name came into Latin from the Greek *Aphro*, a shortened form of Aphrodite, the goddess of love.
5. *The Canterbury Tales*, by Geoffrey Chaucer. It is written in what is known as Middle English.
6. May: 'For it giveth unto all lovers courage, that lusty month of May.'
7. June, the traditional month for marriage, is consecrated to Juno, while July is dedicated to Julius Caesar. The name was suggested by Mark Antony as it was Caesar's birthday month, and it came into use in the same year as Caesar was assassinated.
8. It was first published as *August 1914*, but was later re-titled *The Guns of August*. (World War I became general in August 1914.) The name of the month came from Augustus Caesar, otherwise known as Octavian, the first Roman emperor, and the adopted son and heir of Julius Caesar.
9. *Knickerbocker Holiday*, by Maxwell Anderson and Kurt Weill.
10. Because the Roman New Year began with the month of March.

MOTORING

1. What nineteenth-century development transformed the manufacturing of cars?
2. Which country is credited with producing the first successful motor cars?
3. The phrase 'flying teapot' was affectionately given to which early car?
4. The first competitive event for cars was held in France in 1894 – it was a time trial rather than a true race. Between what two cities was it run, and who was the winner?
5. If a country banned all colours except pink for cars, what would it be?
6. What position in the German Daimler company was held by Mercedes, whose name was borne by its cars from 1901 onwards?
7. What were the initials of Rolls, and the Christian name of Royce?
8. What does drag racing involve?
9. Name the Ford car which was introduced with great fanfare and became the flop of the fifties.
10. Who was the first British driver to win the World Drivers' Championship?

MOTORING

1. The internal-combustion engine.
2. Germany. In 1885 both Karl Benz and Gottlieb Daimler patented cars of this type.
3. The Stanley Steamer, a steam-powered vehicle.
4. From Paris to Rouen. The winner was the Comte de Dion, in a steam car which covered the 79 miles (127 km) at an average speed of 11.6 mph (18.6 km/h).
5. A pink car nation.
6. None. Mercedes was the ten-year-old daughter of Count Emil Jellinek, Austro-Hungarian Consul-General in Nice, who in 1901 was given the concession for the sale of Daimler cars in France, Belgium, Austria-Hungary and America. It is not known whether he induced Daimler to use the name Mercedes out of family pride, or because he thought it would help to get round anti-German feelings in the important French market.
7. Rolls was (the Honourable) C. S. Rolls, and Royce was (Sir) Henry Royce. Their full names were Charles Stewart Rolls and Frederick Henry Royce.
8. Acceleration tests with extremely powerful cars over a quarter-mile track.
9. The Edsel, named after the father of Henry Ford II.
10. Mike Hawthorn, in 1957.

MYTHOLOGY

1. In the Trojan War, what ruse did the Greeks employ to enter the city of Troy?
2. What are the great texts of Icelandic mythology called?
3. What are talaria, and who wore them?
4. Who was Europa?
5. A certain sea god, who had the power to change shapes, gives us what adjective which applies to anyone who changes his mind or opinions easily, to suit the circumstances?
6. Who was the nymph whose unrequited love for Narcissus caused her to pine away until nothing but her voice remained?
7. Can you describe the particular piece of equipment that Procrustes used on his victims to make them measure up?
8. Which god is usually depicted playing a syrinx, or shepherd's pipe?
9. Who were the Aesir?
10. Can you name five of the nine Muses and the art or science over which each presided?

MYTHOLOGY

1. They built a large, hollow wooden horse in which a small group of warriors was concealed. At night, after the Trojans had taken the horse within the city walls, the warriors crept out of the horse, opened the city gates for the Greek army, and Troy was sacked.

2. Eddas.

3. Winged sandals such as those worn by Hermes and Iris, as represented in Greco-Roman painting and sculpture.

4. A Phoenician princess abducted to Crete by Zeus in the guise of a white bull.

5. Protean, from Proteus.

6. Echo.

7. A bed, on which he put all those who fell into his hands. If they were too tall to fit it exactly, he cut them down to size; if they were too short, he stretched them to fit.

8. Pan, the Greek god of woods, fields and flocks, who has a human torso with goat's horns, ears and legs. The word 'panic' derives from Pan, who could arouse terror in lonely places.

9. The gods of Norse mythology, from the Old Norse, plural of *áss*, meaning 'god'. They were thirteen in number, led by Odin, the All-father.

10. Calliope, epic poetry; Clio, history; Erato, love poetry; Euterpe, music and lyric poetry; Melpomene, tragedy; Polyhymnia, sacred poetry; Terpsichore, choral song and dance; Thalia, comedy and pastoral poetry; Urania, astronomy.

NAMES ON THE MAP

1. After whom is the Caribbean Sea named?
2. What prompted the Italian explorer Amerigo Vespucci, when sailing along the northern coast of South America in 1499, to give it the name Venezuela?
3. Apart from both being in Africa, what do the Sahara Desert and Lake Nyasa have in common?
4. Can you name Tamerlane's capital?
5. In 1513 Ponce de León named a group of islands after the Spanish for 'shallow water'. What do we know them as today?
6. What is the only island state in the Caribbean to be named after a church?
7. The former French territory of the Afars and the Issas is now which independent state on the Horn of Africa?
8. The Netherlands means literally what?
9. In 982 Eric the Red sailed west from Iceland and reached the shores of an island further north. Why did he name it Greenland when it was far colder and less hospitable than the island he had left?
10. What European city is famous for a cathedral containing the shrine of the Magi and for a scent it produces?

NAMES ON THE MAP

1. After the fierce Carib Indians, who inhabited the islands of the area.
2. When he encountered native villages built on wooden piles in the shallow water, he was reminded of Venice, and so he named this area 'little Venice', or Venezuela.
3. Since Sahara is from the Arabic word *Sahra,* meaning 'desert', and since Nyasa is a corruption of the Bantu word *nyanza,* meaning 'lake', the Sahara Desert and Lake Nyasa are Desert Desert and Lake Lake, respectively. (Lake Nyasa has been known as Lake Malawi since 1965.)
4. Samarkand.
5. The Bahamas, from the Spanish *baja mar.*
6. Antigua, which Columbus named after Santa Maria Antigua in Seville.
7. Djibouti.
8. Low-lying lands.
9. By giving it a lush-sounding name, he hoped to attract settlers.
10. Cologne, Germany.

OPENERS

Listed below are the opening lines from a number of famous English and American literary works. How many authors and titles can you identify?

1. 'Call me Ishmael.'
2. 'Much have I travell'd in the realms of gold.'
3. 'Come live with me and be my love.'
4. 'He was born with the gift of laughter and a sense that the world was mad.'
5. 'What dire offence from am'rous causes springs.'
6. 'In the year 1878 I took my degree of Doctor of Medicine of the University of London.'
7. 'One thing was certain, that the *white* kitten had had nothing to do with it – it was the black kitten's fault entirely.'
8. 'He did not wear his scarlet coat/For blood and wine are red.'
9. 'I was born in the year 1632, in the city of York, of a good family, though not of that county, my father being a foreigner of Bremen, who settled first at Hull.'
10. 'It is a truth universally acknowledged that a single man in possession of a good fortune must be in want of a wife.'

OPENERS

1. Hermann Melville, *Moby Dick*.
2. John Keats, 'On First Looking into Chapman's Homer'.
3. Christopher Marlowe, 'The Passionate Shepherd to His Love'.
4. Rafael Sabatini, *Scaramouche*.
5. Alexander Pope, *The Rape of the Lock*.
6. Arthur Conan Doyle, *A Study in Scarlet*.
7. Lewis Carroll, *Through the Looking-Glass*.
8. Oscar Wilde, *The Ballad of Reading Gaol*.
9. Daniel Defoe, *Robinson Crusoe*.
10. Jane Austen, *Pride and Prejudice*.

OPERA

1. Can you give the derivation of the word 'opera'?
2. What operas constitute the 'Nibelungen Ring Cycle' of Wagner?
3. Why is the term 'Savoyards' given to the performers in the Gilbert and Sullivan operas?
4. What kind of factory did Carmen work in?
5. Who observed that 'Of all the noises known to man, opera is the most expensive'?
6. In what opera does the aria 'La Donna è Mobile' occur? How would you translate it?
7. Who composed *Die Fledermaus*? *The Merry Widow*?
8. In which opera is there a famous 'Mad Scene'?
9. Name the operas in which these well-known choruses are sung: Anvil, Pilgrims', Soldiers'.
10. In which of Gilbert and Sullivan's works would you hear the following sung:

> 'And everyone will say,
> As you walk your mystic way,
> If this young man expresses himself
> in terms too deep for *me*,
> What a very singularly deep young man
> this deep young man must be!'

OPERA

1. 'Opera' derives from the Latin *opus*, meaning work; *opera*, or works, is the plural. It is a shortened form of the Italian phrase for a musical drama, *opera in musica*.
2. *Das Rheingold, Die Walküre, Götterdämmerung*.
3. Because these operas were originally performed by the D'Oyly Carte Company at the Savoy Theatre in London.
4. A cigarette factory.
5. Molière, the French playwright and actor.
6. *Rigoletto*, by Giuseppe Verdi. 'The lady is fickle.'
7. Johann Strauss, the younger. Franz Lehar.
8. *Lucia di Lammermoor*, by Gaetano Donizetti.
9. *Il Trovatore*, by Verdi. *Tannhäuser*, by Wagner. *Faust*, by Gounod.
10. *Patience*, a light opera ridiculing the 'aesthetic movement'.

PEACE

1. What are the origins of the dove and olive branch as peace symbols?
2. Who used a calumet?
3. Why, according to the Sermon on the Mount, are the peacemakers blessed?
4. Of whom was it said, 'They make a wilderness and call it peace'?
5. Which war was terminated by the peace treaty signed in 1905 at Portsmouth, New Hampshire?
6. What was Henry Ford's contribution to peace during World War I?
7. Many peace treaties were signed in Paris. Those signed there in 1763, 1783, 1856, and 1898 ended which wars?
8. What is ironic about the Nobel Peace Prize, awarded annually to further the cause of international peace?
9. Name the statesman whose confident line 'I believe it is peace for our time,' after he signed the Munich Agreement with Hitler in 1938, came to haunt the advocates of appeasement.
10. Which two armistices were signed in a railway coach in the forest of Compiègne, in France?

PEACE

1. They come from the Book of Genesis in the Bible. There it is said that Noah sent forth a dove from the ark to see if the waters had abated, and the dove returned with an olive leaf in its mouth, indicating that the flood was over and thus that the anger of God was appeased.
2. The North American Indians. It is a long-stemmed, ornamental pipe used for ceremonial purposes and was also known as a 'peace pipe'.
3. 'For they shall be called the children of God.'
4. The Romans. According to Tacitus, it was said by Calgacus to the Caledonians he led before the battle of Mons Graupius in Scotland in AD 83.
5. The Russo-Japanese War.
6. In 1915 he headed a peace expedition to Europe, which proved to be a dismal failure.
7. The Seven Years War, the War of American Independence, the Crimean War, and the Spanish-American War, respectively.
8. Alfred Nobel, a Swedish chemist and manufacturer, invented dynamite, although he later had strong misgivings about the potential use of his invention in warfare.
9. The British Prime Minister Neville Chamberlain.
10. Hitler forced the French to sign the armistice of June 1940 in the same coach where the armistice ending World War I in 1918 was signed. The coach was taken to Germany in World War II and has since disappeared.

PHRASE ORIGINS

Can you give the probable source of the following phrases or expressions?

1. To be taken aback
2. Fit to a T
3. Scarce as hens' teeth
4. In clink
5. Straight from the horse's mouth
6. To lick into shape
7. Flaming youth
8. To pull strings
9. Forlorn hope
10. To show the white feather

PHRASE ORIGINS

1. A sailing ship is taken aback when a change of wind direction presses the sails back against the mast, and progress is halted.
2. This expression comes from the T-square used by draughtsmen for establishing and drawing parallel lines.
3. Pretty scarce, since hens have no teeth.
4. This expression comes from the Clink prison in Southwark which was destroyed in the 1780 Gordon Riots. There is still a Clink Street there.
5. Receiving information in this manner is getting it on the highest authority, in the same way that the only sure way of telling a horse's age is by examining its teeth.
6. In the Middle Ages it was believed that bear-cubs were born shapeless, and had to be licked into shape by their mothers.
7. Not Scott Fitzgerald, but William Shakespeare, when he says in *Hamlet*: 'To flaming youth let virtue be as wax, /And melt in her own fire.'
8. This phrase for using influence to gain an advantage comes directly from the marionette show, where the person behind the curtain pulls strings or wires to control the movement of the puppets.
9. This expression derives from the Dutch words *verloren hoop*, meaning the lost squad or troop. The forlorn hope was originally a body of men specially picked to lead an attack, and particularly to be the first through a breach made in fortifications.
10. This comes from the old sport of cock-fighting. A white feather in a gamecock's tail was an indication that it was not pure-bred, and therefore would not fight so well.

PLANTS AND TREES

1. What is the oldest living thing on earth? The largest?
2. Who was known as the 'Plant Wizard'?
3. Which plant with a branched root thought to resemble the human body is supposed to shriek when it is torn from the earth?
4. The dried bark of a South American evergreen tree provides which drug used in the cure and prevention of malaria?
5. From which country does an ornamental tree called the ginkgo come?
6. Can you give the end products of photosynthesis?
7. How did Socrates meet his end?
8. Which plant, greatly prized by the Chinese for a variety of medicinal purposes, has branched roots resembling the human form?
9. Under which parasitic shrub is kissing encouraged?
10. Which World War I poet concluded his most famous work as follows:

     'Poems are made by fools like me,
     But only God can make a tree.'

PLANTS AND TREES

1. A bristlecone pine named 'Methuselah', in California, with a confirmed age of 4,600 years. A sequoia called 'General Sherman', in California's Sequoia National Park. It stands 270 feet high (83 metres).
2. Luther Burbank, the American horticulturist.
3. The mandrake. In his song 'Go and Catch a Falling Star' John Donne mentions this curiously shaped plant:

    > 'Go, and catch a falling star,
    > Get with child a mandrake root,
    > Tell me, where all past years are,
    > Or who cleft the Devil's foot.'

4. Quinine.
5. China.
6. Carbohydrates and oxygen.
7. Charged with corrupting the youth of Athens, he was forced to drink a poison prepared from the European water hemlock.
8. Ginseng.
9. Mistletoe.
10. Joyce Kilmer, 'Trees'.

PRIME MINISTERS

1. Who is usually regarded as having been Britain's first Prime Minister?
2. Can you name the only Prime Minister to have been assassinated?
3. William Pitt the Younger was the youngest Prime Minister. How old was he when he took office as First Lord of the Treasury in 1783?
4. In this century which two men have held the office of Foreign Secretary after having been Prime Minister?
5. The initials G.O.M. and M.O.G. were both applied to Gladstone. What do they mean?
6. Who was the first chairman of the London County Council in 1889, and later Prime Minister?
7. Many Prime Ministers have accepted an earldom when they relinquished office. What were the full titles taken by Asquith, Lloyd George, Baldwin, and Eden?
8. Who wrote the novel *Savrola, or A Tale of the Revolution in Laurania* and then said, 'I have consistently urged my friends to abstain from reading it'?
9. Which Prime Minister served the longest in the twentieth century?
10. Which Australian State's capital city is named after a British Prime Minister?

PRIME MINISTERS

1. Sir Robert Walpole, who held office from 1721 to 1742.
2. Spencer Perceval in 1812.
3. Twenty-four. (He had been offered the post earlier in the same year, when he was only twenty-three, but had declined.)
4. A. J. Balfour, who was Prime Minister from 1902 to 1905, and Foreign Secretary from 1916 to 1919. Sir Alec Douglas-Home, who was Prime Minister from 1963 to 1964, and Foreign Secretary from 1970 to 1974. (As Earl of Home he had been Foreign Secretary from 1960 to 1963.)
5. Grand Old Man and Murderer of Gordon. (General 'Chinese' Gordon was killed in Khartoum by the forces of the Mahdi in 1885. His death was not avenged until Kitchener defeated the Mahdi's successor at the Battle of Omdurman in 1898.)
6. The Earl of Rosebery (Archibald Philip Primrose).
7. Earl of Oxford and Asquith, Earl Lloyd-George of Dwyfor, Earl Baldwin of Bewdley, and Earl of Avon.
8. Winston S. Churchill.
9. Harold Wilson.
10. Victoria. Melbourne, the State capital, is named after Lord Melbourne, Prime Minister in 1834, and from 1835 to 1841.

RELIGION

1. What is the name of the month during which Moslems fast?
2. Which is the oldest major formal religion still practised?
3. What is the Jewish New Year called?
4. In which tongue did Jesus speak?
5. What does the name Buddha mean?
6. What and where is the Kaaba?
7. Who is eligible for election to the papacy?
8. Who was the only Englishman to become Pope?
9. Can you name the aboriginal religion of Japan which is marked by the veneration of nature spirits and of ancestors?
10. Are the letters IHS a Latin contraction of *Iesus Hominum Salvator,* ' Jesus Saviour of Men', *In Hoc Signo (Vinces),* 'In this sign (thou shall conquer)'; or *In Hac (Cruce) Salus,* 'In this (cross) is salvation'?

RELIGION

1. Ramadan.
2. Hinduism. Its Vedic precursor was brought to India by Aryans about 1500 BC.
3. Rosh ha-Shanah.
4. Aramaic.
5. The Enlightened One.
6. It is the most sacred sanctuary, the centre of the Moslem world, and the chief goal of pilgrimage. It is a small building in the court of the Great Mosque of Mecca, nearly cubic in shape, built to enclose the Black Stone which is the most venerated Moslem object, said to have been given to Abraham by the archangel Gabriel. Followers of Mohammed face towards it when praying.
7. Any baptised Roman Catholic male.
8. Nicholas Breakspear who became Pope Adrian IV in 1154. In the course of his papacy, he authorised Henry II of England's conquest of Ireland.
9. Shinto, which means in Japanese 'the way of the gods'.
10. None of these. IHS is the symbol or monogram of Jesus, from IHSOUS, which is Jesus in Greek capitals.

R.I.P.

1. Who was the first poet to be buried in what was to become Poets' Corner in Westminster Abbey?
2. Whose epitaph is '*Si monumentum requiris, circumspice*' (If you seek his monument, look around), and why is it so apt?
3. In which 'corner of a foreign field that is forever England' is the author of this line buried?
4. What is the significance of the carving of a lion biting the end of a sword on the tomb of King John?
5. Who wrote *The Unquiet Grave*, using the pen-name Palinurus?
6. How are the followers of Alaric I, King of the Visigoths, said to have concealed the place where they buried him after his death while campaigning in southern Italy?
7. Which small island is called 'the burial-place of kings' and is said to contain the remains of 48 Scottish monarchs, including Macbeth and Duncan, the king he murdered?
8. The word 'cenotaph' comes from two Greek words meaning what?
9. According to Ariel in Shakespeare's *The Tempest*, where is Ferdinand's father?
10. Who lies 'under bare Ben Bulben's head' with this epitaph in his own words?

> 'Cast a cold eye
> On life, on death.
> Horseman, pass by!'

R.I.P.

1. Geoffrey Chaucer, because he was a parishioner, not because he was a poet.
2. Sir Christopher Wren's, on his tomb in St Paul's Cathedral, of which he was the architect.
3. Rupert Brooke died aboard ship in 1915 while serving in the Dardanelles Expedition. He is buried on the island of Skiros, one of the Sporades in the Aegean. Above his tomb is a nude male statue symbolising youth.
4. It refers to the Magna Carta, by which the barons curbed the power of the king.
5. Cyril Connolly in 1944.
6. They diverted the river Busento, buried Alaric and his treasures in its bed, and then allowed it to resume its original course. The slaves who did the work were killed to ensure that the secret was kept.
7. Iona, one of the Inner Hebrides, off the western coast of Scotland.
8. Empty tomb.
9. 'Full fathom five thy father lies.'
10. William Butler Yeats. The epitaph is taken from Yeats's poem 'Under Ben Bulben'.

ROCKS

1. To which apostle did Jesus give the nickname of 'Rock'?
2. Describe the fabulous roc.
3. What is the only rock that can be woven?
4. Name the most popular American illustrator of the twentieth century, specialising in scenes from everyday life drawn in a humorous fashion. He was especially associated with covers for the *Saturday Evening Post*.
5. Bill Haley and the Comets reached Number One on the charts in 1955 with a song that was introduced to many through the film *The Blackboard Jungle*. What was its title?
6. What hymn is said to have been written while its author was sheltering from a storm near Cheddar in Somerset?
7. What is a logan-stone?
8. A florid style of ornamentation, characterised by elaborate curved lines and popular in Europe in the eighteenth century, is called what?
9. Can you define 'living stone'?
10. What is the name of the eruptive rock, also called 'blue ground', from which the bulk of the world's diamonds is extracted?

ROCKS

1. Simon Peter (from Greek, *petros*, rock), to whom Jesus said, 'Thou art Peter, and upon this rock I will build my church.'
2. It is a legendary white predatory bird of enormous size and strength which played a large part in the adventures of Sindbad the Sailor, according to Sir Richard Burton's translation of *The Arabian Nights' Entertainments*.
3. Asbestos.
4. Norman Rockwell.
5. 'Rock Around the Clock', which was one of the first original rock 'n' roll hits by a white artist.
6. 'Rock of Ages', by Augustus Montague Toplady.
7. A stone or boulder so finely balanced on its base that it will rock to and fro at a touch.
8. Rococo.
9. 'Living stone' is stone sculpture left in its natural surroundings, as opposed to quarried stone.
10. Kimberlite, named after the city of Kimberley in South Africa.

ROYALTY

1. Which is the oldest ruling house in the world?
2. Where did King Kamehameha rule?
3. Who was the Visigoth king who sacked Rome in AD 410?
4. What relation was Louis XIV to Louis XV?
5. Of which country is King Bhumibol Adulyadej the ruler?
6. Who was Queen Geraldine?
7. Which ruler used a garden for a chessboard and dancing girls as chess pieces?
8. Who met a tragic end at Querétaro in Mexico?
9. Identify Queen Noor.
10. Can you describe the Empress of Blandings?

ROYALTY

1. That of Japan. Emperor Hirohito is the one hundred and twenty-fourth in line from the first Emperor, Jimmu, who is believed to have ruled around the time of Christ.
2. He became in 1810 the first ruler over all the Hawaiian Islands, which were previously governed by warring chiefs.
3. Alaric I.
4. Great-grandfather.
5. Thailand.
6. She was the Hungarian-American countess Geraldine Apponyi, who married King Zog of Albania in 1938.
7. Akbar, Mogul emperor of India in the sixteenth century.
8. Emperor Maximilian of Mexico, who was shot there by the followers of Benito Juárez in 1867. He was the brother of Franz Josef, the Austro-Hungarian monarch.
9. She is the American, Elizabeth Halaby, who was married to King Hussein of Jordan in 1978.
10. The Empress of Blandings was a prize sow belonging to the Earl of Emsworth of Blandings Castle and was described by P. G. Wodehouse in a number of stories as resembling 'a captive balloon with ears and a tail'. She took the Silver Medal at the 87th Annual Shropshire Agricultural Show.

SCIENCE

1. Who invented bifocal glasses?
2. What is the significance of the numbers 2, 10, 18, 36, 54 and 86, which identify a certain aristocratic family? The first three are loners.
3. Who was the chemist noted for his researches with wine, beer and milk?
4. What is the most abundant metal in the earth's crust?
5. After whom is the centigrade scale named?
6. Which law of physics states that for every action there is an equal and opposite reaction?
7. Which metal is named after a goblin?
8. Can you state in words one of Einstein's basic equations, $E = mc^2$? What does it explain?
9. What does the Doppler Effect involve? Explain its significance.
10. Define cloning.

SCIENCE

1. Benjamin Franklin.
2. These are the atomic numbers of the noble gases: helium, neon, argon, krypton, xenon and radon. Of the six, helium, neon and argon never enter into chemical compounds.
3. Louis Pasteur, who gave the world pasteurisation.
4. Aluminium, which accounts for eight per cent of the earth's crust by weight.
5. Anders Celsius, an eighteenth-century Swedish astronomer.
6. Newton's Third Law of Motion.
7. Cobalt, from the German word, *kobold*, 'goblin' of the mines. The ore was so named by the miners because they believed it to be worthless and 'mischievous' when they were smelting and refining other metals.
8. If mass is converted to energy, the energy released (E) equals the mass (m) multiplied by the speed of light (c) squared. This explains how enormous amounts of energy, such as atomic power, are derived from the conversion of very little mass.
9. Observation of the change in wave frequency, as of sound or light, which occurs when the source of the wave and the observer are in motion relative to one another. For example, perceived wave frequency decreases as distance increases. The observation of the Doppler Effect has been employed to determine that the universe is expanding.
10. Cloning (from the Greek *klon*, twig) is asexual, single-parent reproduction in which offspring have the same genetic blueprint as the parent.

SCULPTURE

1. What sister of an emperor inspired one of Canova's most famous nude statues?
2. Who is responsible for the sculpture of the Parthenon?
3. To whom is the statue of Eros in Piccadilly Circus a memorial?
4. Which four American presidents are depicted on Mount Rushmore in South Dakota?
5. Which is the only signed figure by Michelangelo?
6. What nationality was the sculptor Brancusi?
7. Which American sculptor coined a word for what has become an established art form?
8. What are the Elgin Marbles?
9. In which city would you find the celebrated statue, called 'Le Manneken-Pis', of a little boy urinating?
10. Whose statue of St Michael and the Devil is outside the new Coventry Cathedral?

SCULPTURE

1. Pauline Borghese, the sister of Napoleon, who was willing to pose nude because there was a fire in the room.
2. Phidias.
3. Anthony Ashley Cooper, 7th Earl of Shaftesbury, who championed many measures to improve working conditions in factories and mines. The statue, by Alfred Gilbert, forms part of what is properly known as the Shaftesbury Memorial Fountain.
4. George Washington, Thomas Jefferson, Abraham Lincoln, and Theodore Roosevelt.
5. The *Pietà* in St Peter's, in Rome.
6. Rumanian.
7. Alexander Calder, whose mobiles are a type of sculpture consisting of parts that move, especially in response to air currents.
8. They are a collection of sculptures, considered to be some of the finest in the world, taken from the Parthenon in Athens in 1806 by Lord Elgin. They are now in the British Museum in London. Casts of these are in the Metropolitan Museum in New York.
9. Brussels. One story is that the statue was erected by the grateful parents of a lost little boy, whom they found in the pose depicted. Le Manneken-Pis is 17½ inches (45 centimetres) tall and has more than 350 costumes, which are kept at a Brussels museum, the *Maison du Roi*.
10. Sir Jacob Epstein.

SEA CREATURES

1. According to the Bible, what was Jonah swallowed by? How long was he there?
2. Which fish goes through these stages of growth: fry, parr, smolt, grilse, kelt?
3. Who wrote *Moby Dick*, the story of the great white whale? What was the name of the whaling ship, and who were the captain and first mate?
4. Which fish has no bony structure?
5. Which mammal, closely related to the elephant, gave rise to the old mariners' tales of mermaids?
6. The term 'fishwife' has come to mean a termagant, or a coarse, abusive woman. How did this arise?
7. Where would you go to catch sardines? How did they get their name?
8. Where is the valuable 'sperm' of a sperm whale secreted, and for what was it formerly used?
9. Which creature has a large number of blue eyes?
10. The female of which fish stores her eggs in an abdominal pouch on the male?

SEA CREATURES

1. A great fish, not a whale. Three days and three nights.
2. The salmon.
3. Herman Melville. *Pequod*. Ahab and Starbuck.
4. A shark, which is cartilaginous.
5. A manatee, or sea cow.
6. Fishwives were women who sold fish, and they were renowned for their powers of vituperation.
7. There is no such species as a sardine. The sardine tin generally contains young herring, sprats or pilchard. The word 'sardine' is believed to derive from the island of Sardinia.
8. Spermaceti, a waxy substance, is located in the head of the whale and was widely used for making candles.
9. The scallop.
10. The sea horse.

SHERLOCK HOLMES

1. Who was Arthur Conan Doyle's model for Sherlock Holmes? After whom was Holmes named?
2. 'A Scandal in Bohemia' opens with 'To Sherlock Holmes she is always *the* woman.' Can you name her?
3. Describe 'the curious incident of the dog in the night-time'.
4. Where in London was Sir Henry Baskerville staying when the affair of *The Hound of the Baskervilles* began?
5. What connection did Sydney Paget have with the Sherlock Holmes stories?
6. What was the Christian name of Sherlock Holmes's elder brother, and what was the club where he was always to be found from a quarter to five till twenty to eight?
7. Name the American actor who wrote and starred in the play *Sherlock Holmes* early in this century. Who played Billy the pageboy in the London production in 1905?
8. At the start of which story does Dr Watson write of a September equinoctial gale in this fashion: 'As evening drew in the storm grew louder and louder, and the wind cried and sobbed like a child in the chimney.'?
9. What was the title of Holmes's literary effort of his later years?
10. In whose life of Sherlock Holmes does this passage appear: 'So they still live for all that love them well: in a romantic chamber of the heart, in a nostalgic country of the mind, where it is always 1895.'?

SHERLOCK HOLMES

1. Joseph Bell, a consulting surgeon at the Royal Infirmary in Edinburgh, where Doyle took his medical degree. Oliver Wendell Holmes Sr., the American physician and essayist. (Doyle is generally thought to have taken the name 'Sherlock' from a cricketer he had once played against.)
2. Irene Adler.
3. In 'Silver Blaze' this exchange takes place: '"The dog did nothing in the night-time." "That was the curious incident," remarked Sherlock Holmes.'
4. At the Northumberland Hotel. The hotel, formerly the Northumberland Arms, stood at No. 11 Northumberland Street, between Trafalgar Square and the Embankment. The building now houses the Sherlock Holmes Tavern, above which may be seen a replica of the famous rooms at 221B Baker Street.
5. Although not the first, Paget is considered the foremost illustrator of the Holmes stories. His drawings appeared in London's *Strand Magazine*, where he evolved the famous profile we know today.
6. Mycroft; the Diogenes Club.
7. Mr William Gillette and Master Charles Chaplin (to use the form in which their names appeared in the programme).
8. 'The Five Orange Pips.' (Many Sherlockians have conjectured what a child would be doing in a chimney.)
9. *Practical Handbook of Bee Culture with Some Observations upon the Segregation of the Queen*.
10. Vincent Starrett, in *The Private Life of Sherlock Holmes*.

SHIPS AND BOATS

1. Who said to whom: 'There is *nothing* – absolutely nothing – half so much worth doing as simply messing about in boats ... or *with* boats ... In or out of 'em, it doesn't matter.'?
2. What is the difference between a ship and a boat?
3. How many people were on Noah's ark?
4. Which was the largest passenger liner ever built?
5. What was Captain Bligh's mission when in command of the ill-fated *Bounty*? What was his rank?
6. In the following verse who was the lad 'born to be king', and where is Skye?

   'Speed, bonnie boat, like like a bird on the wing.
      Onward, the sailors cry:
   Carry the lad that's born to be king
      Over the sea to Skye'

7. Distinguish between a sloop and a schooner.
8. The 'Blue Riband', for the fastest Atlantic crossing, is held by which ship?
9. Who wrote *Two Years Before the Mast*, a personal narrative which is regarded as an American classic of the days of the sailing ships?
10. For what is Sir Francis Chichester remembered?

SHIPS AND BOATS

1. The Water Rat, to the Mole, in *The Wind in the Willows*, by Kenneth Grahame.
2. A boat is a relatively small craft of a size that might be carried on a ship. The exception to this is the submarine, which traditionally has always been called a boat regardless of size.
3. Eight – Noah and his wife, Noah's three sons, and their wives.
4. RMS. *Queen Elizabeth*. This great ship came to an inglorious end when she caught fire in Hong Kong harbour while being converted into a floating university.
5. To collect breadfruit plants for replanting in the British Caribbean possessions as a source of food. At the time of the famous mutiny Bligh was a thirty-three-year-old lieutenant. He was called captain because he commanded a ship.
6. Bonnie Prince Charlie (Charles Edward Stuart, 'The Young Pretender'). Skye is one of the western isles of Scotland.
7. A sloop has one mast, a schooner more than one.
8. The ss *United States,* which averaged over 35 knots (almost 41 mph, 65 km/h) on her maiden voyage in July 1952. It was said that she was so fireproof that only the piano and the butcher's block were of wood. Withdrawn from service in 1969, the *United States* is being refurbished for her entry into service between the West Coast and the Hawaiian Islands.
9. Richard Henry Dana.
10. Sailing alone around the world in 1966–7 in the Gypsy Moth IV, a 53-foot Bermuda yawl.

SPIES AND TRAITORS

1. In the Bible, who was Rahab?
2. Sir Francis Walsingham performed which important function for Queen Elizabeth I?
3. Whose activities were observed by Pickle the Spy?
4. Who was Sir Leslie Ward?
5. Why is the name of Major Ferdinand Esterhazy infamous?
6. By which name was the exotic dancer Margarete Gertrude MacLeod (*née* Zelle) better known?
7. In what book did Ian Fleming's James Bond first appear?
8. Who was Cicero?
9. Which British naval base was the main target of the group of spies controlled by the man who called himself Gordon Lonsdale?
10. Which famous spy is buried in Westminster Abbey?

SPIES AND TRAITORS

1. The harlot who lodged the two men sent by Joshua to spy 'the land, even Jericho'. – Joshua 2:1.
2. He developed an efficient political spy system for her.
3. Prince Charles Edward Stuart, Bonnie Prince Charlie. Pickle was the pseudonym of Alastair Ruadh MacDonnell, chief of Glengarry. Originally a Jacobite supporter, he was captured by the English and 'turned', spying from 1749 to 1754 on the Young Pretender in exile.
4. 'Spy', the caricaturist especially famous for his drawings of lawyers. He worked for the magazine *Vanity Fair* from 1873 to 1909.
5. Esterhazy was a principal in the Dreyfus Affair in France, during which Captain Alfred Dreyfus was convicted of treason and deported to Devil's Island for life. Esterhazy was the real traitor, who gave to the German military attaché in Paris the *bordereau* (schedule) listing secret French documents.
6. Mata Hari. Dutch-born, she worked as a German spy in World War I, extracting military secrets from high Allied officers who were intimate with her. In 1917 she was arrested and executed by the French. Her stage name Mata Hari means 'Eye of the Morning' in Javanese.
7. *Casino Royale*.
8. It was the code name for the German agent who served as valet to the British Ambassador in Ankara, Turkey, in World War II and photographed many top-secret Allied documents. He was paid £300,000 – in counterfeit bills.
9. Portland, Dorset, home of the Underwater Weapons Establishment. 'Lonsdale', who was really a Russian, and four others were sentenced to varying terms of imprisonment in 1961.
10. Major John André, the British agent in the American Revolution, who negotiated with Benedict Arnold for the betrayal of West Point.

THREE OF A KIND

1. What were the names of Noah's three sons?
2. What does the phrase 'lock, stock and barrel' signify, and to what does it refer?
3. Who had as their motto 'All for one, one for all'? What were their names?
4. Who sailed off one night in a wooden shoe?
5. Name the three rulers who met in 1872 to form the informal alliance called the Three Emperors' League?
6. Can you identify Huey, Dewey, and Louie?
7. What is the name of the Russian sleigh that is drawn by three horses abreast?
8. What three civil servants were greatly burned up by the king but were later promoted?
9. 'Rub-a-dub-dub
   Three men in a tub,
   And who do you think they be?'
10. Who were Julius, Leonard, and Adolph better known as?

THREE OF A KIND

1. Shem, Ham and Japheth.
2. The whole of anything – the lock or firing mechanism, stock, and barrel being the basic parts of a firearm.
3. The Three Musketeers, from the novel of the same name by Alexandre Dumas, *père*, were Athos, Porthos and Aramis.
4. Winken, Blynken and Nod 'Sailed on a river of crystal light/Into a sea of dew,' according to the poem by Eugene Field.
5. The Emperors Franz Josef of Austria, Wilhelm I of Germany and Alexander II of Russia.
6. They are Donald Duck's nephews.
7. A troika.
8. Shadrach, Meshach, and Abednego were cast 'into the midst of a burning fiery furnace' because they would not worship the golden idol built by Nebuchadnezzar, King of Babylon. They were saved by the intervention of an angel of the Lord – Daniel 3:13–30.
9. 'The butcher, the baker, the candlestick-maker.'
10. The Marx brothers – Groucho, Chico, and Harpo.

TIME AND TIDE

1. On what is time calculated throughout the world?
2. Is a neap tide the least or the greatest tide in a lunar month?
3. Who wrote the following epigram?

   'I am a sundial, and I make a botch
   Of what is done far better by a watch.'

4. The hands of clocks or watches in advertisements are generally set at what time?
5. What exactly is 'Big Ben'?
6. What, did the Walrus say, has come, according to Lewis Carroll's *Through the Looking-Glass*?
7. A *tsunami* is usually, although inexactly, known as what?
8. Who declared, in a ringing pamphlet, that 'These are the times that try men's souls.'?
9. Where are the highest tides in the world?
10. Can you name the author of the following lines?

    'The blood-dimmed tide is loosed, and everywhere
    The ceremony of innocence is drowned;
    The best lack all conviction, while the worst
    Are full of passionate intensity.'

TIME AND TIDE

1. *On* the basis of Greenwich Mean Time, which is the mean *solar* time for the prime meridian (0°) at Greenwich, the former home of the Royal Observatory.

2. The least.

3. Hilaire Belloc, *Sonnets and Verse*.

4. Approximately ten past ten, presumably for the sake of symmetry and to frame the manufacturer's name.

5. The hour-bell of the clock in the tower of the Palace of Westminster, in London. Though it is commonly believed to have been named after Sir Benjamin Hall, who was First Commissioner of Works when the bell was hung, more probably it was named after Benjamin Caunt, the 17-stone prize fighter who fought his last fight in 1857.

> '''The time has come,'' the Walrus said,
> "To talk of many things:
> Of shoes – and ships – and sealing-wax –
> Of cabbages – and kings –
> And why the sea is boiling hot –
> And whether pigs have wings.'''

7. A tidal wave. *Tsunami* is the Japanese word for 'harbour wave'. These waves, which cause enormous devastation when they reach land, are generally caused by submarine earthquake or volcanic eruption.

8. Thomas Paine, in *Common Sense*, published in 1776.

9. The Bay of Fundy, in eastern Canada, where the sea level changes by 40 feet (15 metres) during the day.

10. William Butler Yeats. 'The Second Coming'.

TITLES

Give the quotation from which the following titles are taken, naming also the work and the author. (In one instance the source is not a literary one.)

1. *Gone With the Wind*, by Margaret Mitchell
2. *A Handful of Dust*, by Evelyn Waugh
3. *The Little Foxes*, by Lilian Hellman
4. *Remembrance of Things Past (A la recherche du temps perdu)*, by Marcel Proust
5. *My Fair Lady*, by Alan Jay Lerner and Frederick Loewe
6. *Eyeless in Gaza*, by Aldous Huxley
7. *Cakes and Ale*, by W. Somerset Maugham
8. *A Dance to the Music of Time*, by Anthony Powell
9. *Far from the Madding Crowd*, by Thomas Hardy
10. *Arms and the Man*, by George Bernard Shaw

TITLES

1. 'I have forgot much, Cynara! gone with the wind,
   Flung roses, roses riotously with the throng.
   – *Non Sum Qualis Eram Bonae Sub Regno Cynarae*',
   by Ernest Dowson
2. 'I will show you fear in a handful of dust.' – 'The Waste
   Land', by T. S. Eliot
3. 'The little foxes, that spoil the vines',
   – Song of Solomon 2:15
4. 'When to the sessions of sweet silent thought
   I summon up remembrance of things past'
   – Sonnet No. 30, by Shakespeare
5. 'London Bridge is broken down,
   My fair lady.'
   – 'London Bridge' (Anonymous)
6. 'Eyeless in Gaza, at the mill with slaves'
   – 'Samson Agonistes', by John Milton
7. 'Dost thou think, because thou art virtuous, there shall be
   no more cakes and ale?'
   – Shakespeare's *Twelfth Night*, Act II, Scene 3
8. 'A Dance to the Music of Time' is a painting by Nicholas
   Poussin, now in the Wallace Collection, in London.
9. 'Far from the madding crowd's ignoble strife,
   Their sober wishes never learn'd to stray.'
   – 'Elegy Written in a Country Churchyard', by Thomas Gray
10. 'Arms and the man I sing' (*Arma virumque cano*)
    – The Aeneid, by Virgil

TRAVELS AND VOYAGES

1. Which expedition leader first succeeded in circumnavigating the earth in one voyage?
2. Who travelled with Modestine?
3. Can you give a popular derivation of the word 'posh' that arises from a luxurious type of accommodation on a long sea voyage?
4. Which widely-travelled Venetian brought pasta to Italy?
5. Which young Cambridge graduate sailed around the world on board the ten-gun brig HMS *Beagle*?
6. Who was the avaricious old boatman who ferried the unfortunate ones across a river?
7. 'I met a traveller from an antique land ...' is the beginning of which famous poem?
8. What was the name of the surgeon who sailed from England on a series of voyages, starting with the merchant ship *Antelope* in 1699? In the course of his travels he encountered all sorts of people, including some mad scientists trying to extract sunshine from cucumbers. He returned to England with a great admiration for horses.
9. How was the Reform Club at 104/5 Pall Mall, London, connected with a celebrated trip?
10. Why, according to the mediaeval legend, was the Wandering Jew condemned to wander?

1. Not Ferdinand Magellan, but Sir Francis Drake, in a voyage lasting just under three years, from 1577 to 1580. Magellan sailed halfway around on two separate voyages. He was killed by natives in the Philippines on his second voyage, but the expedition continued under Juan Sebastián del Cano, who became the first man to circumnavigate the globe in 1522.

2. Robert Louis Stevenson. Modestine was the donkey of his *Travels with a Donkey in the Cévennes*.

3. It is said that in the days of the British raj, well-heeled passengers on a round trip to India requested choice cabins on the shady side of the ship – that is, 'port out, starboard home', giving us the acronym 'posh'. This, however, must come under the heading of folk etymology as there is no firm evidence that it is true.

4. Marco Polo, after his extensive travels in China in the thirteenth century. Besides pasta he told of asbestos, coal, paper currency, and other phenomena virtually unknown in Europe.

5. Charles Darwin, who held the post of naturalist on the ship. It was on this voyage that he visited the Galapagos Islands, where he found key evidence for his theory of evolution.

6. Charon, who ferried the dead across the Styx, one of the five rivers separating Hades from the land of the living. According to Greek mythology, the passenger paid with the coin left in his mouth when he was buried.

7. 'Oxymandias', by Percy Bysshe Shelley.

8. Lemuel Gulliver, the hero of Jonathan Swift's satiric masterpiece *Gulliver's Travels*.

9. In Jules Verne's story *Around the World in Eighty Days*. It was there that Phileas Fogg began and ended his fabulous trip, and won his wager.

10. He refused to let Christ rest at his door when He was on His way to Calvary, or, according to another version, urged Him to go faster as He was leaving Pilate's Judgment Hall.

WEATHER

1. Who is reputed to have said, 'Everbody talks about the weather, but nobody does anything about it.'?
2. In classical mythology, who was controller of the winds?
3. What was the chief characteristic of the Pleistocene Epoch?
4. Who enquired, 'Where are the snows of yesteryear?'
5. Define isobars.
6. Can you complete the verse beginning, 'Red sky at night …'?
7. How does the Gulf Stream affect the climate?
8. To what was Shelley referring in these lines?

> 'I am the daughter of Earth and Water,
>   And the nursling of the Sky;
> I pass through the pores of the ocean and shores,
>   I change, but I cannot die.'

9. What does the Beaufort Scale measure?
10. Under which Government Ministry does the Meteorological Office come?

WEATHER

1. It has been attributed to Mark Twain, although the line is not found in his published works. It does, however, appear in the editorial column of the *Hartford Courant*, written by his friend Charles Dudley Warner.
2. Aeolus.
3. The alternate appearance and recession of northern glaciation, also called the Ice Age.
4. François Villon, in 'Ballade des dames du temps jadis'.
5. They are lines on a map connecting points of equal barometric pressure.
6. 'Red sky at night, sailors delight –
   Red sky at morning, sailors take warning.'
7. Its warming waters raise the average temperature of areas in the higher latitudes.
8. A cloud.
9. The Beaufort Scale, devised by Admiral Beaufort of the Royal Navy, is a scale by which successive ranges of wind velocities are assigned numbers.
10. The Ministry of Defence.

WEIGHTS AND MEASURES

1. What unit of measurement is used to measure the height of a horse?
2. Explain why 'lb' is the abbreviation for pound.
3. On a thermometer when are the Fahrenheit and centigrade readings identical?
4. Do you know the derivation of the word 'ton'? What is the difference between a short or American ton and a long ton?
5. In the metric system, approximately what does one litre of water weigh?
6. A cubit is an ancient unit of linear measurement mentioned often in the Bible. In what fashion was it determined?
7. 'Full fathom five' is how deep?
8. What is the capacity of a ten-gallon hat?
9. What is the metric unit called a stere used to measure?
10. Can you name the dark comedy by Shakespeare that was set in Vienna?

WEIGHTS AND MEASURES

1. A hand, equal to four inches.
2. From the Latin *libra*, scales – hence 'pound'.
3. At -40^0.
4. It derives from the Old English *tunne*, meaning a cask or measure of wine. A short ton is 2,000 pounds and a long ton is 2,240 pounds.
5. One kilogram, which is about 2.2 pounds.
6. Originally it was the length of the forearm from the tip of the middle finger to the elbow, or about 17-22 inches.
7. 30 feet.
8. Less than a gallon.
9. Timber. A stere is a cubic metre.
10. *Measure for Measure*.

WOMEN

1. Who was the world's first woman Prime Minister?
2. What female American Indian was a huge social success in London?
3. To be a quean was to be what in the sixteenth and seventeenth centuries?
4. Who was married to two kings and was the dominant figure in the politics, culture, and social life of twelfth-century Europe?
5. What is a 'Messalina'?
6. What was the original meaning of a gossip?
7. What were the Christian names of Mrs Pankhurst's three daughters who helped her in her fight for women's suffrage?
8. Who was Dulcinea?
9. What etymological connection does the word 'lady' have with bread?
10. In June 1893, a brutal double axe-murder in Fall River, Massachusetts, inspired the following bit of doggerel:

    'Lizzie Borden took an axe
    And gave her mother forty whacks;
    When she saw what she had done
    She gave her father forty-one.'

What was the verdict in the trial of Lizzie Borden?

WOMEN

1. Mrs Sirimavo Bandaranaike, who became Prime Minister of Ceylon (now Sri Lanka) in 1960.
2. Pocahontas.
3. A bold or ill-behaved woman; a jade; a strumpet.
4. Eleanor of Aquitaine. She was married to Louis VII of France and Henry II of England.
5. An oversexed woman. Messalina was the third wife of the Roman Emperor Claudius I.
6. Among the early English, a *godsibb* was a sponsor at a baptism, the *god* part of the word standing for 'God', and *sibb* meaning 'kinsman'. The word later came to mean a 'boon companion' and then gossip as we know the term.
7. Christabel, Sylvia, and Adela.
8. The imaginary love of Don Quixote. Dulcinea del Toboso was the name he gave to the peasant girl Alonza Lorenzo.
9. In Anglo-Saxon times the most important duty of the housewife was the making of bread, and she was called a *hlaefdige*, or 'bread-kneader', which subsequently evolved into 'lady'. In the 1600s, however, the word fell into disrepute, and to be a lady was largely to be a lady of pleasure. Now it has come into its own again as a term of decency.
10. Not guilty.

WORLD WAR II

1. On 3 September 1939, the day Britain declared war on Germany, the signal 'Winston is back' was flashed to all ships and bases of the Royal Navy. What did this signify?

2. In the early part of the war, during England's darkest hours, President Roosevelt sent a note to Prime Minister Churchill quoting some lines from Longfellow and adding, 'I think this verse applies to your people as it does to us.' What were the lines?

3. The battle of El Alamein was one of the turning points in the war. In what country did it take place, and who were the opposing commanders?

4. Who, according to the British, was 'overpaid, oversexed and over here'?

5. What major operations had the code names Barbarossa and Overlord?

6. Which battle in the Pacific in June 1942 is considered to be one of the decisive Allied victories of the war?

7. Describe 'Pluto' and the 'Mulberries', which were used to great advantage during the Normandy landings.

8. Who was the Supreme Allied Commander South-East Asia from 1943 to 1946?

9. Can you translate the word *kamikaze*, the name given to the suicidal crash-attack planes used in desperation by the Japanese at the end of the war?

10. What were the three British four-engined aircraft which were the mainstay of Royal Air Force Bomber Command from 1941 to 1945?

WORLD WAR II

1. That Winston Churchill had been appointed First Lord of the Admiralty, the same position he held at the outbreak of World War I.

2.
   'Sail on, O Ship of State!
   'Sail on, O Union, strong and great!
   Humanity with all its fears,
   With all the hopes of future years,
   Is hanging breathless on thy fate!'

3. The western Egyptian desert. Rommel and Montgomery. Of this battle Churchill was to write, 'Before Alamein we never had a victory. After Alamein we never had a defeat.'

4. The American G.I. in Britain. He sometimes retorted that the British soldier was 'underpaid, undersexed, and under Eisenhower'.

5. Barbarossa was the German invasion of Russia in 1941 (Frederick I of Germany was called this because of his red beard). Overlord stood for the cross-Channel liberation of France in 1944.

6. The Battle of Midway, which was fought chiefly with aircraft, resulted in the destruction of these Japanese aircraft carriers, crippling the Japanese navy.

7. 'Pluto', Pipe Line Under The Ocean, was the code name for the submarine pipelines for oil. 'Mulberries' were large synthetic harbours built on the beach which enabled ships to unload a vast amount of supplies before the major French Channel ports had been captured.

8. Admiral Lord Louis Mountbatten, later Earl Mountbatten of Burma.

9. Divine Wind, after the wind that had destroyed a Mongol armada in the thirteenth century.

10. The Avro Lancaster, the Handley Page Halifax, and the Short Stirling.

X CERTIFICATE

1. How did *X* come into being as a symbol for an unknown quantity?
2. What was the name of King Arthur's sword?
3. Xerox, the trademark for a photocopying process, is derived from what?
4. Who was Xerxes?
5. Define xenophobia.
6. In the verse from Longfellow below what was the 'strange device'?

> 'The shades of night were falling fast,
> As through an Alpine village passed
> A youth who bore, 'mid snow and ice,
> A banner with the strange device –'

7. What is an *ex post facto* law?
8. What was the name of the Jesuit missionary who was known as the Apostle of the Indies?
9. Who was Xanthippe?
10. What is the meaning of 'xd' shown against the quoted price of a company share?

X CERTIFICATE

1. It came into Europe from Arabia, where the word *shei*, meaning 'thing', was used for an unknown quantity. This was transcribed as *xei* and later simplified to *X*. A famous example is X-rays, which were so named by their discoverer, Röntgen, because he did not understand their nature.
2. Excalibur.
3. Xerography, a dry photocopying process, from the Greek *xeros*, meaning dry, and *graphos*, written.
4. He was the King of Persia who, in the fifth century BC, defeated Leonidas at Thermopylae and went on to pillage Athens. He returned to Persia after the Greeks destroyed his fleet at Salamis.
5. Fear or hatred of strangers or foreigners.
6. A banner on which was written the single word 'Excelsior!'
7. Any law enacted with a retrospective effect, so as, for example, to make an act criminal which was not so at the time it was committed.
8. St Francis Xavier, who in the sixteenth century took Christianity to India, the Malay Archipelago, and Japan.
9. Socrates' wife, whose name is synonymous with a conjugal scold. Shakespeare refers to her in *The Taming of the Shrew*.
10. Ex-dividend; i.e., purchasing the share at that price does not entitle the buyer to a dividend already declared but not yet paid.

YIDDISH

Can you give the English equivalent of the following?

1. Shlemiel
2. Shlimazel
3. Chutzpah
4. Megillah
5. Goy
6. Meshuga
7. Shmaltz
8. Nebbish
9. Shiksa
10. Shalom

YIDDISH

1. A fool or clumsy bungler; one who spills the soup.
2. An even bigger fool, a luckless person; one on whom the shlemiel spills the soup.
3. Brazenness, unmitigated gall. One who kills his parents and asks for mercy on the grounds that he is an orphan has chutzpah.
4. A long complex story or explanation.
5. A Gentile.
6. Crazy.
7. Literally, cooking fat; excessive sentimentality.
8. A weak, helpless, or pathetic person.
9. Literally, an abomination; a non-Jewish girl; also implies an impious or wild Jewish girl.
10. Peace; hello; good-bye.

ENDINGS

1. At what famous moment in history did who say: *'Voilà le commencement de la fin.'* (This is the beginning of the end.)'

2. According to T.S. Eliot in 'The Hollow Men', how does the world end?

3. The tune of 'Till the End of Time' is based on which masterwork?

4. Which novel ends 'Which of us is happy in this world? Which of us has his desire? or, having it, is satisfied? – Come, children, let us shut up the box and the puppets, for our play is played out.'?

5. What is the meaning of 'eschatology'?

6. 'Great is the art of beginning, but greater the art of ending' was written by which noted American poet?

7. Who said and in what work: 'Laughter is not at all a bad beginning for a friendship, and it is far the best ending for one'?

8. Can you give the last two lines of the song 'Taking a Chance on Love'?

9. Why does the word 'penultimate' belong here?

10. To cover an awkward moment when the curtain failed to drop at the end of a show, what was Ethel Barrymore's famous ad-lib?

ENDINGS

1. Talleyrand, on the announcement of Napoleon's Pyrrhic victory at Borodino in 1812.
2. 'Not with a bang but a whimper.'
3. Chopin's 'Polonaise in A Flat'.
4. *Vanity Fair*, by William Makepeace Thackeray.
5. The doctrine of last or final matters, such as death, resurrection, immortality, judgment.
6. Longfellow, 'Elegiac Verse'.
7. Oscar Wilde, in *The Picture of Dorian Gray*.
8. 'We'll have a happy ending now,
   Taking a chance on love.'
9. Because it means 'next to last' (Latin *paene*, almost, and *ultimus*, last).
10. 'That's all there is. There isn't any more.'